Get That Job

I0469921

The Ultimate Guide

How to secure that interview, answer tough questions and negotiate more pay.

By Terry Melaugh

Copyright © 2013 Terry Melaugh

Disclaimer

This is an information guide. It is not intended as a substitute for legal or other professional services. While every effort has been made to make this guide accurate, it may contain typographical or content errors. The information expressed herein is the opinion of the author. The author and publisher shall have no responsibility or liability with respect to any loss or damaged caused, or alleged to be caused, by the information or the application of the information contained in this guide.

Table of Contents

Introduction

Introduction

The goal posts have moved

Historically less attention was paid to job interview preparation. Job security was the norm. Employees often remained with the one employer for life. There was less competition for vacancies.

The last decade has seen a dramatic change in the job market. In the current economic climate more applicants are chasing fewer positions. Job security for life no longer exists. The modern workforce is more insecure than its predecessors. Economic conditions force workers to change jobs more often. Neither employers nor employees feel obliged to commit to a long term working relationship.

Employers now demand a much higher standard of interview performance. Companies have become more selective and demanding in their recruitment processes. Job hunters have been forced to improve their performance. There is increased competition for vacancies due to higher levels of unemployment and increased job turnover.

It is no longer enough to talk about your experience and skills in order to secure the job offer. You must also supply concise examples of your accomplishments. You must demonstrate your suitability. You must indicate how your skills can be used to bring savings to your new employer.

Redundancy has become a common place occurrence. Even established companies are going under. In these challenging conditions you must adapt a winning job search strategy in order to gain an advantage over the competition.

How this book will help you succeed

By following the advice in this book anyone can improve their chances of securing a job offer. Whether applying for your first job, climbing the career ladder or returning to work after a career break, this book is for you. It will show you how to stand out from the pack as the clear and obvious choice to fill the vacancy.

This book explains the recruitment process from the employer's perspective. It outlines how the short listing and selection process works from the company's viewpoint. It reveals the employer's thinking and game plan. It explains what causes employers to reject candidates. This knowledge will enable you to avoid the common pitfalls that cause candidates to be rejected at each and every stage of the process.

This book explains the winning tactics to employ. It points out the characteristics that employers desire. Understanding what employers want enables you to tailor your application accordingly. Once you grasp the fundamental rules of the game, you will be able to secure the job offer you want.

Preparation

The key to all success is preparation. This book covers the job search and application process. It gives advice on preparing for interview, passing tests and performing at the interview and assessment centres. You will be guided through every stage of the application process. You will be shown how to make a successful application and get that vital first interview.

Preparation involves finding out about the company and the vacancy. It also involves analysing your own skills and closely matching them to the employer's specified requirements.

Excelling at the interview

Most jobs are allocated on the basis of interview performance. If you can succeed at interview you will be able to secure better paying jobs and improve your career prospects.

Advice is given on how to answer the most common interview questions, including the tricky ones. Sample answers are provided, which you can adapt to your own circumstances. You should read these examples and construct answers based on your own experiences. You will then be less apprehensive and nervous at the interview. Just like any test, it is much easier to pass an interview if you know the questions in advance and receive a set of mock answers. You will know what to expect, and how to react.

This book offers advice on how to perform at interview. You will be given tips on what to say and what not to say. Once you appreciate the interviewer's perspective you will know what he requires. You will be able to match your skills to his needs. You will be able to sell yourself with confidence.

You will be advised on your appearance and your behaviour. You will learn to control your body language and how to create the right impression. You will be shown how to look out for tell tale signs from the interviewer's body language. You will know which type of behaviour will lead to job offers. You will understand which actions automatically lead to rejection.

The interview is basically a match making process. The candidate who makes the best impression at the interview often receives the job offer. This may not necessarily be the best person for the job. You must learn to sell your skills. You must convince the interviewer of your suitability. You must pass scrutiny.

Advice is given on the right questions to ask to improve your chances of selection. You will also be shown how to carry out a post-interview analysis. This will enable you to perform even better the next time. Finally you will receive advice to guide you through any difficult negotiations in order to secure the job offer you want.

Lack of preparation and interview pitfalls

This book will highlight the most common interview pitfalls. You will be shown how to avoid them. Screening interviews are used to reject candidates one at a time until only a few remain. Those who are rejected fall for the traps that have been laid. Those who survive know how to recognise and side step these traps.

If you receive an invite to interview the employer believes, from your application, that you meet all the essential selection criteria for the job. To save time and money applicants who lack the minimum experience will be filtered out before the interview stage. Providing you can avoid the interview pitfalls, the job offer is within your grasp. Failure at this stage is usually the result of poor preparation.

Many candidates fail to prepare. They do no groundwork beyond preparing their CV. They have not bothered to find out enough about the company and the vacancy. They are flying by the seat of their pants. This becomes immediately apparent to the interviewers.

Unprepared candidates fail to utilise the limited time available. They fail to sell their skills, knowledge and suitability for the position. They regret that they have not made the right impression at the interview. They wish that they had added some relevant point. They regret not being asked the right questions. They fail to realise that they should have rehearsed everything they wanted to say in advance. They should have included all of their main selling points in their answers. Regardless of how well the interviewer performed they should have made their own case for being selected. They are the seller and the interviewer is the buyer. It is their job to pitch the sale.

Chapter 1. How the selection process works

Before applying for a job you must first understand how the
selection process works. You need to appreciate the ground rules
of the game from the employer's perspective. This insight will help
you prepare your application. It will ensure that you are short listed
to attend the job interview.

Considering the vacancy

There are a number of stages in the selection process. First of all,
the company looks at why the vacancy has come about. Why did
the last person leave the position? Was the job too demanding?
Does it need to be reviewed? They will carry out an exit interview
with the previous job holder if he gives his notice.

The company will then assess the job. Is it still relevant in its
current format? There may be other employees whose workload
has reduced due to changes in demand. Perhaps the job can be split
up? The various tasks could be assigned to under utilised
employees. Maybe the job could be automated?

Deciding to proceed

If the job is essential, then management will sign off on the need to
fill the vacancy. The next stage is to analyse the job in detail.

The job description

For a new position the company will draw up a job description.
The job description lists the main tasks, duties and responsibilities
involved in carrying out the job. The following information is
usually included:

- Job title.
- Organisation and department details.
- Job title of the immediate supervisor.
- Job titles of the staff reporting to the job holder.

- The main functions and objectives of the job.
- The main duties and key responsibilities.
- Salary and main terms and conditions of employment.
- The scope of the job.
- Statement of whether job is full time, part time, temporary or permanent.
- Any special requirements, such as the need to work shifts.
- Performance and career prospects.

An updated job description is useful in three ways:

- It helps the company prepare job specific interview questions.
- It can be used to help prepare the job advertisement.
- It can be sent to job applicants.

The person specification

The next stage is to prepare a person specification. This document is sometimes referred to as a job specification. The person specification describes the qualities that the job holder should possess to ensure a satisfactory level of job performance. It lists the competencies required in terms of:

- Educational qualifications and training.
- Knowledge and intelligence.
- Experience and previous responsibility level.
- Specific job related skills.
- Personal attributes such as leadership, teamwork and self-motivation.

The person specification should list the essential competencies. These are the minimum requirements needed in order to be short listed for interview. These are a prerequisite. The person specification should also list the desirable competencies an ideal candidate might possess. The company must pitch these requirements at the level of the job in terms of the main duties.

For existing jobs the company will update both the job description and person specification. They will include any changes in the job since these documents were last revised.

Considering internal applicants

The company will first look to fill vacancy internally. There are several reasons for doing this:

- It is less expensive to fill the position internally.
- There is less risk associated with appointing an internal candidate.
- The company can reallocate labour away from areas that are contracting.
- It allows the company to develop its staff.
- An internal promotion policy helps improve employee morale.
- It reduces turnover in the long run.

Checking on-file candidates

In some cases a suitable internal applicant may not be available. Perhaps the company has already advertised internally and did not get any suitable applicants. Sometimes the company wants an injection of new ideas from outside. If this is the case the company will next consider the list of recent applicants for similar positions. Their applications should still be on-file. Filling the vacancy this way saves advertising and short listing costs. If there are no suitable applicant details on-file, the company will opt to advertise the position.

The job advertisement

The job advertisement is drawn up using the information in the person specification and the job description. Advertisements vary in format, style and content. However, a typical advertisement will contain most of the following information:

- The company name, unless recruitment is being carried out by an agency.

- Company details such as size, location and main products.
- A brief mission statement.
- Job title.
- Job location.
- Job authority level.
- Main responsibilities.
- Essential and desirable selection criteria.
- Salary details.
- Main conditions of employment.
- Shift pattern and working hours.
- Initial training and probation details.
- Promotion prospects.
- Details of how to reply to the vacancy.
- The deadline for receipt of applications.

Targeting the advertisement

The more specific the advertisement is, the easier it is for the person reading it to determine if the job is suitable for them. This is why it is better to include salary details. Pay is the main determining factor for most candidates. Details like salary, location and shift pattern make it possible for the reader to self-select. The reader will opt out if the conditions are not suitable. This saves the company having to de-select a large number of unsuitable applicants.

Sometimes a single advertisement will include several different vacancies. If so, each vacancy will be given a unique reference number. You must quote this reference number when responding to the application.

Placement of advertisements

Some jobs will be advertised internally as well as externally. Internal advertisements are usually posted on company notice boards. External advertisements may be placed through various media such as:

- Newspapers.

- Trade magazines.
- Company website.
- Radio and television.
- Employment agencies.
- Recruitment websites.
- Job centres.
- Executive search consultants.
- Education or training establishments.

Short listing

Interviewing is an expensive process. It ties up a lot of time and resources. Only a select few applicants will be invited to the interview process. The company will wait until the closing date has passed. They will then sift through the received applications. They will draw up a short list of people they wish to interview. All other applicants will be rejected.

Each applicant's competencies will be compared with the essential requirements. This results in a long list of applicants possessing the minimum criteria.

If there are more applicants on this list than the company wishes to interview, the process will be repeated. The bar will be raised by including some of the desirable criteria. Only applicants with the additional specified desirable criteria will be included. If the list is still too long, the process will be repeated once more. Additional desirable criteria will be added until the list of applicants is cut to the desired number. This will result in the final short list of applicants who will be invited to interview.

Sometimes there are not enough candidates possessing the minimum requirements. This might happen for senior or specialised roles. The company faces two alternatives. Either re-advertise the position, or reduce the minimum requirements. The latter choice is the cheaper option. Relaxed minimum requirements are applied to the current applicant list. If the company lowers the required standard, they may offer a lower starting salary.

The interviewer's preparation

The interviewer will prepare himself in the following way. He will:

- Familiarise himself with the job.
- Get the immediate supervisor's views on the job requirements.
- Draw up a list of core questions to ask each candidate at interview.
- Study each short listed application in advance.
- Highlight any omissions, gaps or inconsistencies in these applications.
- List further probing questions for each candidate.
- Prepare an interview assessment sheet to score all applicants on the same basic criteria.

A separate assessment sheet will be used for each candidate. The interviewer will make brief notes on each candidate's answers during the interview. He will complete the scoring immediately after the interview, when the details are fresh in his mind. More details of how the interviewer will do this, is given in Chapter 14.

Interview format

There are a number of different interview formats. The simplest format is a short interview, conducted by a single interviewer. The most complex is perhaps a two day selection course carried out at an assessment centre. This might consist of panel interviews, group discussions, in-tray exercises, presentations, tests, role playing and problem solving exercises.

The interview format will depend on the level and nature of the job involved. For example, management vacancies involve a more complex selection process.

The purpose of the interview

The main purpose of the interview is to find the best person for the job. Each candidate will be asked a series of identical questions, plus some follow up questions. The aim is to assess the candidate's suitability. This is done by matching his competencies with the job requirements from the person specification.

When a job offer is agreed, both parties should be satisfied with the outcome. In a perfect scenario an ideal match will have been made. Both parties will benefit from the relationship. However firms often fail to select the best candidate. Likewise applicants regularly accept job offers that don't turn out as expected.

This situation can be avoided if both parties prepare in advance. Each side should have acquired and shared enough information to come to the right decision. There is an onus on both parties to ask the correct questions. They should listen to and consider the responses.

Selection tests

Candidates may be required to sit selection tests as part of the short listing process. Depending on what is tested, this may occur before or after the first interview stage. However final selection will hinge on performance at interview. More information on selection tests is included in Chapter 10.

The medical examination

You may be asked to take a pre-employment medical examination. The job offer may be conditional on you passing the medical examination. Medical examinations are carried out for a number of reasons.

- To ensure that the candidate is fit enough for the job.
- To identify how the job may be altered to help the candidate to perform to the required standard.
- To provide a baseline health profile.

A reading of your baseline health profile can protect the firm from future claims. If, for example, you already have partial hearing loss this will be noted. It forewarns the company of the need to periodically check your condition, or refer you to your own doctor.

The medical examiner may record potential risks in terms of future sickness, absence or injury.

You do not need to be extremely fit to pass the examination. Your health just needs to be commensurate with your age. So an older person would not be expected to have the same quality of hearing as a younger candidate. Medical examinations may include:

- Hearing and eyesight tests.
- Blood pressure.
- Height and weight.
- Pulmonary or lung function tests.
- A general physical examination.

You may have to give urine or blood samples. You may be questioned on your medical history.

You may be asked to attend a medical examination for a number of reasons:

- It may be a statutory requirement for that type of job. The job may be demanding, or the employee might be expected to work in isolation. You may be expected to drive or ferry passengers.
- A baseline examination is required if you will be exposed to noise or need to wear respiratory equipment.
- The results of your pre-employment medical questionnaire might indicate a problem requiring further investigation.

Do not become anxious about attending a medical examination. If your health is reasonable you should pass the examination. If you fail a medical examination ask for the details. Contact your own doctor to discuss the issue. If a company nurse has carried out the examination, request a second opinion from the company doctor. The doctor may recommend that it is safe to hire you to work under specified conditions.

If you fail the medical examination you may not be offered the job. This might occur because:

- You are physically or mentally incapable of carrying out the job in a safe manner.
- You have an existing condition that might be exacerbated by the job.
- You have a disability, such as poor hearing, which could pose a risk to your safety and that of work colleagues.

If you fail the medical you could offer to sign a disclaimer relating to your condition. This might persuade the employer to hire you. They might offer you a different job where your condition will not hamper your safety.

Other pre-employment checks

You may be applying for a job where you will be working with, or in close proximity to, children or vulnerable adults. In this case your details will be checked against the Criminal Records Bureau (CRB). An enhanced check would be carried out under these circumstances.

Standard CRB checks are also required for certain professional occupations such as legal and financial jobs. The standard check will be for convictions, cautions, reprimands and warnings contained on the Police National Computer.

Foreign born nationals will be asked to prove their place of birth and hence eligibility to work in the UK. The Asylum and Immigration Act, 1996, makes it a criminal offence for employers to employ workers from certain countries. European Union inhabitants are entitled to work in any member country.

Offering the job

References are usually taken up before a job offer is made. If these are satisfactory, the first choice candidate will be made an offer. This will usually be accepted, sometimes after a period of negotiation. One or two reserve candidates may be retained in case

the first choice withdraws. All other candidates will receive letters
of rejection.

Chapter 2. Analysing your personal skill set

The absolute need to analyse your personal skills

Do not begin your job search until you have analysed your personal skills, strengths and weaknesses. You need to understand the tasks that you like doing best. You must appreciate where your natural talents lie. There are two reasons you must do this:

- To assess which type of job will suit you best.
- To sell these skills at interview.

Get professional careers advice. It is best to find a job which utilises your talents, with an environment in which you can flourish. In the long run this will make you happier and more likely to succeed.

Will the job suit you?

Before you begin your job search you must first appreciate what you want from a job. Do you want the job to fit in with a clearly defined career path? Do you simply want a part time job to earn some extra cash?

For your long term well being, you need a working environment in which you will be happy.

The danger of not understanding your career requirements

Unhappiness at work is one of the leading contributors to stress. Remaining in a stressful environment for prolonged periods can have detrimental effects on your health.

If you take an unsuitable job there are several likely outcomes. In the short term you will not contribute as much as you should. You will gain less satisfaction and acquire fewer skills. In the longer term you will probably choose to leave. In your anxiety to leave you may take the first available opportunity. This could be a slightly better option, but still not entirely suitable. So the cycle continues. Picking the wrong jobs hampers progression in your career.

Many people stumble from one job to another. They are not sure what they want from a job. They just realise that they haven't found it yet. They accept jobs that do not suit them. They then move to something not quite as bad. They waste valuable time flitting from one unsuitable position to another. Time they could have used to acquire new skills and build a career. This type of person often gives up before they ever find their ideal job. They never achieve contentment in their working environment.

Flitting from one unrelated position to another does not look impressive on your CV.

Transferable skills

Transferable skills are versatile skills that can be used in a number of different roles. These skills are acquired throughout life from experiences at school, university, previous jobs, hobbies, sports and family life. Transferable skills make it easier to transition into and succeed in any new role. These basic skills are required in every job to some degree or other.

Self-knowledge is critical in understanding which type of job will suit you best. You can acquire this knowledge by analysing the current status of your transferable skills.

Analysing your transferable skills

You need to analyse your personal skills using the approach the interviewer will take. The questions you should consider are listed below. These questions are grouped into categories. These are the same categories that employers use to assess your interview performance.

There are no absolute answers to these questions. Our behaviour varies depending on circumstances. It is influenced by mood, physical and mental health and outside pressures. However you should know approximately where you lie on a particular scale. You might be optimistic at times and pessimistic at others. You will, however, have a tendency towards one trait or the other.

You need to be aware of your skill level in each area. You should then work on how to improve these skills. Taking self-assessment tests will help you determine the level of your skills.

Once you have analysed your skills, match them to the advertised job requirements. This is relatively easy if applying for a job in the same career sector. If you are looking to change careers it takes a little more thought and planning. Your CV will have to be altered in order to emphasise your transferable skills.

Employers hire people based on their attitude rather than having a perfect match in work related skills. They look for signs of self-awareness and a desire to improve personal skills.

Leadership skills

Leadership skills are an asset that all employers value. A leader ensures that his team works towards common company goals. Consider the following:

- Do you like to be in charge?
- Do you prefer others to look to you for leadership?
- Do you like to tell others what to do?
- Are you self-motivated? Can you motivate others?
- Do you have long terms goals?
- Do you set and communicate clear goals.
- Do you embrace change, or do you prefer routine?
- Are you genuinely interested in the company and your team?
- Can you be trusted to lead a team?
- Can you look after the needs of your team?
- Can you lead by example?
- Can you supervise others effectively?
- Can you resolve difficulties and maintain a harmonious working atmosphere?

- Do you accept full responsibility for achieving results?
- Do you understand what makes people tick?
- Do you delegate work where possible?
- Are you prepared to discipline others?
- Can you assemble and get the best out of your team?
- Do you regularly praise others?
- Can you persevere, overcome setbacks and achieve results

Leadership skills can be applied in various roles at all levels from team leader, supervisor, manager, director up to CEO.

Analytical skills

- Are you quick to grasp the fundamentals of a problem?
- Are you good at absorbing new information?
- Can you discriminate between the important factors and the less relevant?
- Do you have an enquiring nature?
- Can you grasp complex issues?
- Can you estimate probabilities?
- Can you analyse data?
- Have you good observation skills?

Communication - written and oral

- Have you good oral communication skills?
- Can you explain things easily?
- Are you confident and coherent in your speech?
- Are you a good listener?
- Are you good at written communication?
- Do you have good presentation skills?
- Can you write effective reports?

Influencing skills

- Can you put an argument forward in a logical way?
- Can you get others to come round to your point of view?
- Can you agree on common ground if there is a difference of opinion?

- Are you assertive or submissive?
- Are you prepared to compromise?
- Can you negotiate the best possible deal?

Planning and organising

- Have you got effective planning skills?
- Can you manage yourself?
- Have you effective time management skills?
- Are you generally impulsive or do you like to plan things in advance?
- Do you take a longer term view?

Decision Making

- Can you make decisions easily?
- Can you reach decisions independently?
- Do you possess sound judgement?
- Do you trust in your own capabilities?
- Can you estimate risks?
- Do you tend to keep an open mind until you have assessed all the facts?
- Are you prepared to alter the plan when conditions change?
- Do you often change your mind?

Education

- What subjects did you enjoy most at school or college? Why?
- Do you want a career that utilises your qualifications?
- Did you perform well at school, college or university?
- Should you consider further education or part time courses?
- Should you acquire additional qualifications to enhance your career prospects?

Intelligence

- Are you good with words and language?
- Have you an aptitude for figures, shapes and symbols?

- What is your preferred learning style? Hands on, listening, reading, imitating?
- Do you use logic to find solutions?
- Can you think out of the box?
- Do you analyse performance and learn from experiences?
- Can you quickly grasp new concepts?
- Do you keep an open mind?
- Do you continually strive to learn new things?

Interpersonal skills

Interpersonal skills are valued by all employers. Teams can only succeed by working to common goals in a harmonious atmosphere. People need to get on well with one another. There needs to be an understanding of the other person's viewpoint. Any conflict will detract from the overall performance of the team. Conflict leads to increased staff turnover and hence additional costs to the company.

Employees with strong interpersonal skills are more successful. They learn from their interactions with others. They analyse what went well and what did not in these interactions. They take corrective action. Their working and personal relationships improve.

Consider the following:

- Can you communicate clearly?
- Do you raise immediate objections, or do you show tact?
- Can you settle differences without antagonising others?
- Do you heed instructions and feedback from others?
- Can you pick up on the moods, feelings and emotions of others?
- Are you interested in people and what makes them tick?
- Are you willing to take on extra duties to help the team out?
- Can you discern the motives of others?
- Can you influence the behaviour of others?
- Can you encourage others to do their share of the work?
- Will others help you out in emergencies?
- Are you sensitive to the feelings and needs of others?
- Do you feel concerned about the welfare of others?

- Do others come to you with their concerns?
- Are you good at explaining things?
- Do you share your knowledge with others?
- Do you acknowledge the work of the team?
- Do you mix well with people?

If you have good people skills consider a career in teaching, nursing, medicine, social care, selling or retail.

Attention to detail and completion of tasks

- Do you double check your work?
- Are you prone to errors, or do you seldom make mistakes?
- Can you concentrate for long periods?
- Do you like to finish things yourself?
- Would you prefer others to complete the details?
- Are you a perfectionist?

Disposition and temperament

- Do you worry a lot?
- Do you tend to be patient or impatient?
- Are you careful or careless?
- Are you self-motivated?
- Do you recognise your own limitations?
- Are you more of an optimist than a pessimist?
- Are you generally enthusiastic?
- Are you introverted or extroverted?
- Are you generally serious, or do you enjoy having fun?
- Do your emotions cloud your judgement?
- Are you self-confident, or do you doubt your abilities?
- Are you generally relaxed, or do you tend to be hyperactive?
- Do you complain a lot?
- Do you hide your emotions, or do you prefer to let them show?
- Are you prone to aggression?
- Are you emotionally stable?

Initiative

- Are you an ideas person?
- Do you show initiative often?
- Are you a creative person?
- Do you volunteer for tasks?
- Do you make the most of your opportunities?

Drive and perseverance

- Are you a competitive person?
- Do you stick to your goals despite setbacks?
- Are you energetic?
- Do you set your own targets?
- Do you prefer to develop the ideas of others?
- Do you work on improving your personal skills?
- Have you developed a long term career plan?

Recognition and rewards

- Do you seek public recognition?
- How important is social status to you?
- Do you want a high status job?
- Do you want to attain a high standard of living?
- How important is material reward to you?

Entrepreneurial skills

- Do you develop new ideas and take them to fruition?
- Would you prefer to work for yourself?
- Would you like to run your own business?
- Do you respond to opportunities?
- Are you willing to take risks?
- Are you resourceful?

Management style

- Are you over-critical of others?
- Are you judgemental of others?
- Are you autocratic, democratic, persuasive, and consultative or laissez faire?

Job related skills

In addition to your personal skills, consider the job related skills that you have acquired during your career.

Administration skills

These basic skills are required in the engine house of all businesses, the office.

- Forecasting.
- Budgeting.
- Auditing.
- Stock taking.
- Managing money.
- Working with plans and diagrams.
- Setting and meeting deadlines
- Collating data.
- Evaluating and analysing data.
- Extracting important information
- Preparing reports.
- Computing skills.
- Time management.
- Organising.
- Planning.

If you are skilled at manipulating data consider clerical, secretarial, administrative, computing, or general office work.

Practical, mechanical or engineering skills.

- Hand, eye coordination.
- Building or construction.
- Operating machinery.
- Driving.
- Mechanical ability.
- Fault finding.

- Fixing or maintaining machinery.
- Assembling machinery or equipment.
- Woodwork or other crafts.

People with this skill set should consider a practical trade such as electrician, carpenter, plumber, joiner or mechanic. They should consider working in engineering, maintenance, construction, servicing or production environments.

Creative Skills

- Thinking strategically.
- Problem solving.
- Verbal skills.
- Written skills.
- Being creative.
- Expressive.
- Artistic.
- Musical ability.
- Dance.
- Designing processes or things.

If you are particularly creative consider the arts, design, product development, science or research.

Decide what motivates you

Next consider the type of job you would enjoy. Consider the following issues:

- Is status and recognition important to me?
- What level of responsibility do I want?
- Which skills do I want to employ?
- Am I looking for a challenge or do I prefer routine?
- Do I want a creative or inventive job?
- Do I need variety in my work?
- Am I looking for a change of direction?
- Do I want to use my own initiative?

- Do I want to improve my expertise?
- Do I want continual learning?
- Do I need job security?
- Do I want to work on my own or as part of a team?
- Do I want to utilise interpersonal skills?
- Would I like to work with customers or clients?
- How much would I like to earn?
- Do I want to help others?
- Do I want to help society?
- Do I want to start a business?

List your strengths and weaknesses

List the positive and negative aspects of your character. Refer to this list and add to it over time.

Work to your strengths

Having established your strengths, look at ways to utilise them at work. Volunteer for additional duties that allow you to use these talents. This will enable you to develop additional experience. This experience will stand you in good stead. You will be able to talk about it at interviews. It will also improve your chances of promotion.

Have a development plan

List the areas you want to improve. Develop a plan to bring about this improvement. Review this plan regularly. Work on rectifying some of your negative characteristics. Look at how others behave and handle situations at work and elsewhere. Look at how people interact. Notice what gets results. Notice what leads to dissent and conflict. Try to emulate the behaviour that yields results. Talk about how you work to improve your interpersonal skills when asked about your weaknesses at interview.

Chapter 3. The job search

Changing Direction in your career

People decide to change career direction for several reasons. Their current job may be in a declining industry. Their job may be under threat due to automation. They may have been the victim of redundancy. They may now want a less demanding career to get them through to retirement. They may want a greater degree of job satisfaction. They may wish to become self-employed. They may just be dissatisfied in their current job and fancy a change.

You need to:

- Research the new career and sector.
- Think about what you want.
- Consider getting new qualifications.
- Analyse what you like and dislike about your current job.
- Analyse your personal skills, strengths and weaknesses.
- List all your transferable skills.
- Keep your options as wide and open as possible.
- Understand the barriers to entry.
- Use your network and contacts to make introductions.
- Contact the real decision makers.
- By-pass personnel departments. They automatically reject unqualified applications.
- Remain in your existing job until you have secured a new position.
- Phase in self-employment by starting off in your spare time. Build up your business before leaving your current job.
- Stay focussed and determined.

Consider if you are just running away from something. It might be better to tackle the problem head on. Do not confuse problems in your personal life with the desire for career change.

Be prepared for setbacks. Career change is a time consuming process.

Take into account economic conditions

In recessionary times employers are more selective. A high unemployment level increases the number of applicants. Employers attempt to reduce this number by moving criteria from the desirable list to the essential list. They know they can secure better qualified candidates and offer them lower salaries.

Changing career direction is challenging when the economy is buoyant. It is even more difficult in times of recession. Employers are unwilling to hire unqualified employees from a different sector. They are reluctant to spend scarce resources training them to the required standard. After all, there is an over abundance of suitably qualified applicants out there already. Take this into account when deciding on your suitability for an advertised role.

Target jobs for which you are qualified in your own career sector. Select a job at your current experience level and work on being promoted internally.

Be realistic in your goals

Be realistic in your expectations. It is acceptable to apply for a position one step up the ladder. When transferring to a different industry, it is difficult to move up a level at the same time. It is more realistic to move at the same level.

It is a waste of time to try to take two steps up the career ladder in a single move. You are unlikely to be short listed. If the job level is unclear from the advertisement, ring the personnel department for assistance.

If you do not have all or most of the listed essential criteria, skip to the next vacancy.

Consider working for smaller companies

Companies with less than 250 employees account for 99.9% of businesses in the UK and employ 60% of the workforce. Small and medium sized companies can offer many benefits:

- There are fewer applicants per vacancy.
- There are twice as many vacancies available.
- Smaller firms will consider your application more carefully.
- You will be given broader responsibilities.
- There is greater variety in the work.
- There is a greater range of learning.
- You gain a higher profile much more quickly.
- You have a greater individual impact on operations.
- You can get more rapid promotion.
- There is limited hierarchy, so your views will be heard at the top.
- There is less bureaucracy, so you get things done quicker.
- There can be a family run atmosphere.
- There is more team spirit.
- There is a greater level of job satisfaction.
- There is ease of communication.
- The environment is more challenging.
- You will get a better grounding if you plan to start your own business.

People working for smaller firms have a greater level of job satisfaction. They can see the end result of their endeavours. They feel they can approach their boss directly. They can have problems resolved immediately. They tend to be more committed to their jobs and their company. They have lower stress levels at work. Smaller business owners know the value of their staff. They treat them as individuals. They like to keep valued employees who produce results.

The qualities that smaller companies desire in applicants

- Ability to learn quickly on the job.
- A practical and common-sense approach.
- Flexibility.
- Willingness and ability to acquire a variety of skills.
- Ability to work unaided.

- Ability to work well under pressure.
- Ability to produce results.
- Relevant qualifications or experience.

If you have spent a lot of time working for larger companies, smaller firms may be reluctant to hire you. They will fear that you do not appreciate the needs of a small business. Will you struggle to look after several departments at the same time?

The benefits of larger corporations

Larger companies can be more difficult to get into. They are usually swamped with applications. They will have rigorous selection procedures, including attendance at assessment centres. They have a narrow view of the type of personality they want for a given role.

Larger firms offer a number of advantages:

- Higher entry salary levels.
- Greater job security.
- Added credibility to your CV.
- More structured training.
- Sponsorship for recognised qualifications.
- Larger budgets to control.
- More people to supervise.
- Documented, recognised procedures.
- Additional perks.
- More opportunity to specialise.

Consider placements using a temporary agency

Temporary agencies help place job seekers with companies. There are a number of advantages to using a temporary agency:

- You gain access to unadvertised jobs.
- There is often the chance of securing a permanent job.
- They are a useful first contact if you are moving to a new region.
- They facilitate your job search.

- If you do not have a lot of work experience, they can help get you started.
- You can register with more than one agency at the same time.

Apprenticeship programs

Apprenticeships were traditionally available in trades such as engineering, construction and crafts. This has broadened out into many other areas. Apprenticeships are now available in arts, media, agriculture, horticulture, health, leisure, business administration and areas of management and sales. There are now more than 200 apprenticeship programs available in England covering 1200 different job roles.

Apprenticeships are open to all age groups above 16 years old, not in full time education. Apprentices earn a wage, working alongside experienced staff while learning new skills. They usually attend specific training courses, often on a weekly day release basis. They study for exams and Nationally Vocational Qualifications. (NVQs).

Apprenticeships are usually offered at different levels. Salary is paid on an increasing scale as training progresses. It takes a number of years to complete the apprenticeship program, depending on the nature and level of apprenticeships. However at the end of this the apprentice will have gained valuable skills, experience and qualifications. Many will have secured full time employment with a sponsoring employer.

Finding out where vacancies exist

Job vacancies can be posted in a number of areas:

- Internet search engines.
- Job boards.
- Company website.
- Company notice boards.
- School or university careers office.
- Libraries.

- Job centres.
- Recruitment agencies.
- Recruitment agency websites.
- Job fairs.
- National Newspapers.
- Local newspapers.
- Trade journals and technical press.
- Local radio and television.
- Networking.
- LinkedIn
- Vacancies listed at the employer's premises.

Internet search engines

You can use internet search engines to find job vacancies from a number of sources. These include company websites, trade and professional organisations, career guidance sites and recruitment sites. The internet is the favoured medium for advertising vacancies. It is rapidly becoming the preferred medium for accepting applications.

Job boards

Job boards are websites which host vacancies placed by recruitment agencies and employers. Specialised job boards cater for a particular profession or industry. Other sites cover a particular region. Some are national.

Job boards have job search engines facilitating the location of suitable vacancies. You can narrow your search by geographic location, job description, key word, salary level or industry sector. Your search result may link you to the agency or employer's website.

There is usually a facility to upload your CV. Job boards offer additional services such as job alerts on suitable vacancies.

Company website

Most companies will post job vacancies on their websites. The advantage is that the cost is minimal. Company websites include information on the company, its history, main products, location, workforce, mission statement and industry trends.

Company notice boards

Internal vacancies are usually posted on company notice boards. Check these regularly. It is often easier to gain promotion internally than seek a better job elsewhere.

School or university careers advisory service

University careers advisory services provide the following services and information:

- Advertising vacancies.
- Helping with initial career choice.
- Highlighting opportunities in the UK and abroad.
- Providing internet access.
- Providing career and professional reference books.
- Providing employer details.
- Hosting of milk round or first stage interviews.
- Organising recruitment fairs.
- Advice on postgraduate and further studies.
- Advice on training opportunities.
- Job search advice.
- Advice on filling application forms.
- CV preparation.
- Interview skills coaching.
- Mock interviews.
- Assessment centre preparation.
- Interactive workshops.
- Advice on taking tests.
- Occupational career talks.

The service is free to students and recent graduates who can visit any local university careers advisory service.

The careers advisory service publishes two newsletters each fortnight, *Graduate Opportunities* and *Prospects Today*. These give details of vacancies in the UK and Republic of Ireland.

Libraries

Libraries will hold trade or business directories. They often hold copies of trade journals. Libraries also offer internet access.

Job centres

Tel: 08456 060 234 Job search helpline
www.direct.gov.uk

Job centres are government run agencies which advertise vacancies and provide assistance in obtaining employment. Jobcentre Plus is a part of the Department for Work and Pensions in the UK. Local firms advertise positions at Jobcentre Plus offices. The service is free to employers and job seekers. Job centres can provide employers with candidates fairly quickly. However the available pool is mainly drawn from the unemployed.

Job centres offer advice on training initiatives and special grants. They rune job clubs aimed at getting longer term unemployed back into work.

Recruitment agencies

Some recruitment agencies specialise in clerical, secretarial and administrative positions. Others specialise in engineering, maintenance and technical positions. Agencies tend to fill part-time and temporary positions. Agencies offer the following advantages:

- They are familiar with the local job market.
- They have contacts with employers.
- They know the latest vacancies.
- They deal with unadvertised vacancies.

Recruitment agencies often advertise the vacancy and carry out first screening interviews.

Arrange to meet a consultant at a suitable local agency. Fill in any application forms and leave your CV. Describe the type of work you are looking for and briefly cover your experience. Treat any such meeting as you would a job interview. The consultant will make an assessment. They will decide which employers they are willing to recommend you to.

You can use a couple of agencies at the same time. However you do not want two agencies sending your CV to the same employer.

Follow up with each agency at agreed intervals. Get feedback on employer reaction to your CV. If an agency keeps sending you leads on the wrong type of job, arrange to meet the consultant again. Explain exactly the type of work you are seeking. If they do not have the right employer contacts, move on to a different agency.

If they organise an interview, ask them about the company and the vacancy. The employer will often have explained their detailed requirements to the consultant.

You may have been unsuccessful at an interview arranged by a recruitment consultant. The consultant may be able to get feedback from the company on your performance. This will be invaluable advice in preparation for future interviews.

Recruitment agency websites

Recruitment agency websites may be general or specific to a particular industry or profession. They upload vacancies from local employers.

Job fairs

Job fairs are organised by university careers offices, local councils, job centres and recruitment agencies. A number of employers set up stall on a given day at a suitable local venue. Each will have human resources and other department managers present. They bring along advertising literature, company brochures, free samples and display samples of their products.

Job fairs provide:

- An indication of the available jobs.
- A chance to meet employers in a less rigid environment.
- A better chance to ask questions than at an interview.
- An opportunity to make contacts.

In order to get the most out of your job fair experience:

- Find out in advance which companies will be present.
- Research those companies that are of interest.
- Prepare as if you were attending an interview.
- Dress as you would for an interview.
- Approach each stand when it is quieter.
- Aim for five minutes to talk to the employer.
- Use your research to impress the employer.
- Ask sensible questions.
- Bring your CV and leave it with the employer.
- Get their business cards.
- Get an application form and any background information.
- Follow up with a letter to each individual you spoke to.

National newspapers

National newspapers advertise for particular jobs sectors on the same specific day each week. For example the Guardian will advertise education jobs on a Tuesday and health jobs on a Wednesday.

- The Guardian.
- The Times.
- The Financial Times.
- The Daily Telegraph.
- The Independent.

National newspapers host on-line recruitment boards where you can search for jobs by key sectors. You can upload your CV for employers to view. You can register your email address for job alerts.

Local newspapers

Local newspapers cover local vacancies. Daily papers advertise jobs on a particular day each week. Local papers write features on companies relocating to or expanding in their particular area. Local newspapers also provide information on job fairs, open days, general business reports and employer profiles.

Trade journals and technical press

Trade magazines are available at local libraries. They cover most industries. There are trade magazines for professions such as accountancy, financial services, health care, insurance and legal sectors.

Vacancies are often advertised in trade or technical press. This allows employers to target their advertisement to qualified applicants. Companies advertise for specialised roles through this medium.

Trade journals provide articles on the latest technology, industry trends, industry leaders, product development and research. Interviewers will be aware of such developments and interested in their potential. The ability to answer questions on these issues will influence interviewers.

Local radio and television

The main disadvantage of using radio or television advertising is that the message is transitory. It depends on the right listener or viewer having tuned in at the right time. Advertisements need to be repeated and run for a period of time to get a suitable response. Television is the most expensive medium but it has the greatest impact. It is favoured for general recruitment campaigns by bodies such as the armed forces.

Networking

Friends, colleagues or family may know of vacancies that exist where they work.

If applying for a vacancy you can contact someone you know who works with the company. Ask them what it is like to work for the company. Ask about the department where the vacancy occurs. Try to get a feel for how things get done in the company. Ask them about employee morale and the results of any staff satisfaction surveys.

If you do not know anyone working for the company then use social networking sites to get in contact with a current or past employee.

LinkedIn

LinkedIn is the largest professional networking service on the internet. It has more than 200 million registered users in over 200 countries. Registered users can create an on-line professional profile. They also have a list of people or connections with whom they are linked professionally. These connections are linked to other second degree connections and so on. Your connections can recommend a suitable vacancy based on your profile and knowledge from their connections. Be careful to screen who you add as connections. Check out their Facebook site. The list of connections is visible to prospective employers.

Prospective employers can list jobs and view user profiles. Users can view company profiles and their latest vacancy listings. They can bookmark jobs in which they are interested. Many recruitment agencies use LinkedIn when head-hunting prospective employees.

Social media sites

Employers use social media sites to post or tweet vacancies. They can target particular groups using this method. Facebook has a job board offering employers a formal platform on which to post vacancies. Social networking sites offer huge audiences for employers. This provides a readymade cheap method of advertising.

Employers view user profiles as part of their screening process, just before deciding to offer interviews. They will screen candidates out on the basis of negative aspects of their profile, including:

- Negative behaviour.
- Inappropriate language or photographs.
- Negative comments on their existing employer.
- Disclosure of confidential company information.

Do not have any material of this sort on your main page. Do not leave your privacy settings open. This would enable others to post inappropriate material on your wall or profile. Any tweets or comments can leave a permanent record. Employers can eavesdrop on your conversations. You need to anticipate the company carrying out on-line research on prospective candidates.

Vacancies listed at the employer's premises.

You may be seeking work with an organisation that is open to the public. If so, visit it yourself as part of your research. Examples include hotels, pubs, garages, supermarkets or shops. They often post vacancies near the entrance and you can usually collect an application form on site.

Talk to employees serving the public. This will give you a feel for the job and the company.

Chapter 4. Before you apply

Before you apply for a job you need to study:

- The job requirements.
- The company.
- Your competencies
- How closely your competencies match the specified requirements.
- The best way to demonstrate your suitability in your application.

This will enable you to target your application to the precise job requirements.

The job requirements

Sources of information on the job requirements are the:

- Job advertisement.
- Job description.
- Person specification.

The job advertisement

The job advertisement contains some basic information about the company. This might include their location, main business or products and the reason for recruiting at this stage. The advertisement might also specify the number of vacancies.

The job advertisement will specify the essential and desirable criteria for selection. It will also give details on the location, authority level, main responsibilities and conditions of employment. It may indicate salary details and promotion prospects. The advertisement should indicate the shift pattern, working hours and initial training and probation details.

The job advert usually gives details of a contact person who can provide further information about the vacancy. If not, you can ring the personnel department.

The personnel department

Find out everything you can about the company before attending the interview. Ring up the personnel department. Ask for background information on the company. Ask for a copy of the job description and person specification.

Think about the type of person the company wants to hire. The advertisement should contain the essential and desirable criteria for selection. Additional information will be provided in the job description and the person specification. Consider the level of responsibility the job holder will have and the scope of the job.

Specific company information to gather

You can get information on the company from the personnel department, the company's website and general on-line searches. Obtain the answers to as many of the following questions as possible:

Company size, structure and organisation

- When was the company founded?
- What size is the company?
- Is it a private or public company?
- How many people work for the company?
- Where are the company headquarters?
- Where are the main locations?
- What are the main company divisions and subsidiaries?
- What is the function of the main departments?
- Who is the Chairman or Managing Director?
- What is the management structure?
- Who are the major shareholders?
- What type of customers does the company supply?

Company performance

- Is the company expanding or contracting?
- Is the industry growing or declining?
- Is the company financially secure?
- Is the company profitable?
- Who are the major competitors?
- What differentiates the company from its competitors?
- Is the company under threat from changes in technology, market demands or competitive activity?
- Has the company won any industry awards?
- Has the company secured any major contracts recently?
- Are there any pending mergers, acquisitions or joint ventures?
- Are there any pending redundancies?
- Have there been any recent setbacks?
- What are the company's main priorities?

Company services and products

- What are the company's main products and services?
- Is the company developing new products or services?
- Which products or services are most profitable?
- How does the company's products compare with those of its competitors?
- In which products is the company investing most?
- What type of manufacturing facilities does the company have?
- Is the company planning to open any new facilities?

Company culture

- Does the company encourage employee participation?
- Does the company consult with its employees?
- Does the company carry out employee satisfaction surveys?
- What training facilities does the company provide?
- Does the company have an internal promotion policy?
- What is the company mission statement?
- What are the core company values?
- What kind of reputation does the company have?
- Is the company family friendly?

- Does the company promote equality for female employees?
- How does the company treat older employees?

Would you feel comfortable working with the company? Will you fit in with the company culture? Will you conform to the expected norm? Is there scope for future promotion?

Published annual accounts

Get hold of a set of published company accounts, available from Company's House in the UK. The director statement will outline future developments and indicate the financial stability of the firm. It will also indicate where the company is expanding or investing.

Suitable working conditions

Consider the working conditions associated with the job. You will be spending a considerable amount of time at work. You need to be happy in the working environment. Study the advertisement and consider the following:

- Where is the vacancy located?
- How long is the commute to and from work?
- What are the shift patterns?
- Is the job permanent or temporary?
- Is the job full-time or part-time?
- What is the rate of pay?
- Are there likely to be additional benefits?
- What is the level of responsibility?
- Is it an office job, a production job, or outdoor work?
- Will the environment by warm, cold, noisy or otherwise uncomfortable?
- Will you have to wear special uniforms or protective clothing?
- Will the job make excessive demands on your personal life?

 All of these factors will be important when deciding if you want the job.

Consider your suitability

Do you meet the selection criteria for the job? Make a list of each of the essential criteria. Alongside each requirement, note some practical examples of your experience which demonstrate your competency. Repeat the process for the desirable criteria.

If you meet all the essential criteria and any of the desirable criteria, your application will have a good chance of being short listed.

If you are applying for a promotion, or a job in a slightly different role, you may lack some of essential criteria. In this case, you will have difficulty being short listed for interview. You must stress equivalent qualifications or experiences in your CV and covering letter. Use your covering letter to point out any additional desirable skills you possess. If you are applying for a specialised or senior role, where there are few fully qualified candidates, you might get lucky and be short listed for interview.

Do not waste your time if you are not qualified

If your skills are not a close enough match to the job requirements, the whole process should stop at this stage. By continuing you will be wasting your time and efforts on a lost cause. If applying to a lower skilled job, you will not be considered if you lack any of the specified essential criteria. Just move on and concentrate on a vacancy for which you are better suited.

Chapter 5. The curriculum vitae (CV)

Job advertisements often require you to submit a curriculum vitae or CV to support your application. Curriculum vitae is a Latin term. It means 'the course of your life.' Your CV summarises your personal details and career to date. It is a personal marketing or sales tool. It portrays your own personal brand. You must design your CV to sell your skills, abilities and experiences in the most positive light. You must include your unique selling point.

The purpose of the CV

The purpose of the CV is to obtain a job interview. It is a door opener. You have control over what to include and what to leave out of your CV. You must be selective in what you include. You only need enough information to get the interview. The CV should arouse curiosity. The aim is to persuade the reader to invite you to interview.

A well constructed CV will:

- Draw attention to your availability.
- Create a professional impression.
- Outline your relevant skills and experience.
- Indicate how closely your skills match the job requirements.
- Highlight your personal competencies.
- Summarise what you can contribute to the firm.

First impressions

First impressions are critical. You will not get a second chance to make a first impression!
A well presented CV will ensure that you will get off to a great start at interview.

CV Format

Unlike an application form a CV is unrestricted in content, format and style of presentation. You are in complete control of how the document looks.

Your CV should be formatted as follows:

- Typed and neatly tabulated.
- Use black ink with regular fonts.
- Print on good quality A4 white paper.
- Use laser quality print.
- Keep length to 2 one-sided sheets.
- Total should be about 600 words.
- Use clear, simple and concise language.
- It should be easy to read and interpret.
- Use short simple statements.
- Avoid long paragraphs.
- Arrange the contents in clear sections.

Remember you may have to send your CV by e-mail. Avoid any fancy design features. These might become scrambled when opened with a different version of word processing software.

Contents

Your CV should only contain relevant facts. Include the following information about yourself:

- Name and contact details.
- Personal profile.
- Key skills.
- Career summary.
- Education and training.
- Personal details.

Name and contact details

Include your name and contact details at the start of your CV. The person scanning it needs to immediately identify the owner. Include your:

- First name and surname (family name) in that order.
- Full postal address, including postcode.
- Home and mobile telephone number, including full STD code.
- E-mail address.

Make sure you list the correct telephone contact details. Arrange to use an answering service. If you have recorded your own automated answering message, make sure that it is businesslike. Employers often ring up to arrange a time and date for interview.

Personal profile

A personal profile is a personal statement contained in one paragraph. It outlines your main selling points. It is the most important part of your CV. You need to take great care in composing it. The purpose is to pique the reader's interest and make them delve further.

Summarise in 60 to 80 words your:

- Current job function including seniority level.
- Most relevant experience.
- Key work related skills and strengths.
- Areas of expertise.
- Achievements to date.
- Key personal qualities and interpersonal skills.
- Immediate career aspirations in terms of what you can offer.

Target your personal profile to the vacancy. Concentrate on your recent experience. Highlight your strengths and potential. Indicate your suitability for the role. You need to distil down to your unique selling point.

The profile can be set out in bullet points. Write it in the third person as if describing someone else. You can use phrases rather than full sentences.

Draw up your personal profile after you have completed the rest of your CV. At that stage you will know the best points to include in this section. The remainder of your CV should justify the selling points in your personal profile.

Key Skills

Match this section of your CV to the specified job requirements. Only include information that helps you get the job. Indicate how you have all the essential criteria. Include any desirable criteria you also possess.

Present any additional relevant skills as a unique selling point. However be careful not to appear overqualified. Pitch your sale to the level of the vacancy.

Chronological career summary

It is usual practice to use a reverse chronological format for your career details. Start with your current or most recent position and work backwards. Give more detail on your most recent or most senior role. Include progressively less information as you work your way back to your earlier, more junior, roles. The employer is only interested in the last ten years of your experience.

In each case give brief details of:

- Your employer, name and location of the company and business type.
- Starting and finishing dates, e.g. 1996 – 2000.
- Job title.
- A brief summary of your functional responsibilities.
- Your main accomplishments.

Include only relevant and supporting information. Draw attention to the most relevant job in a covering letter. Avoid any unexplained gaps in your dates. Interviewers seek explanation for these. Cover up small gaps by including only the year in starting and finishing dates. Avoid longer gaps by listing study, travel, voluntary work, self-employment or family commitments.

Specify the number of people you supervised and the level of your budget responsibility. Quantify your accomplishments in terms of the savings or benefits you brought to the company.

Functional career layout

A functional or competency based CV summarises the skills you acquired throughout your career. It is better to use a functional career layout when:

- Your most recent job is not relevant to the advertised vacancy.
- You have had several unrelated jobs.
- There are obvious gaps in your career history.
- Your relevant skills have been acquired in a number of roles.
- You want to alter career direction.

Education and training

Include educational details in reverse chronological order. Begin with your most important qualifications and work backwards, listing relevant details such as:

- Secondary schools, colleges and universities attended, including dates.
- Academic achievements – degree, A-Levels, GCSEs, etc.
- Distinctions, scholarships, merits or prizes.
- Professional and technical qualifications.
- Ongoing professional development or vocational training.
- Positions of responsibility, such as school prefect or class councillor.
- Computer skills.
- Language skills.
- Professional membership.

Include grades for degrees. Do not include grades for A Levels or GCSEs unless a specified grade is required. You may choose to ignore this advice if you got all A or A* grades.

The more work experience you have, the less important education becomes to the employer. If you are an experienced applicant, summarise your educational qualifications. Include them towards the end of your CV. If applying for a professional job, include the relevant qualifications.

If you are a recent school leaver, or graduate, include details of all subjects and exam results to date. List educational details prominently on the first page of your CV. Include details of projects undertaken and research papers written. Your academic results are taken as an indication of likely job performance.

Do not list exams you failed. Just give details of the subjects you passed. Supply those exam certificates that match the subjects you listed. The interviewer will only check the results you include in your CV. They may only check those qualifications described as essential in the job advertisement.

Only include relevant training courses you attended.

Personal details

In this section include:

- Interests and hobbies, if you do not have much work experience.
- Driving license details.
- A note that references can be provided.
- Details of any work permits, if relevant.

Make sure that you include only genuine interests. You must know enough about each topic to talk about it at interview.

First and subsequent drafts

A lot of time and effort is needed to produce a good quality CV. However the effort will reap rewards. A well prepared CV will ensure that you get invited to interview.

Include all of your personal skills and work experience in your first draft. Save this as a first reference for subsequent job applications. This is your standard CV. If you have a lot of experience this version might be four or five pages long.

Polishing your CV

Producing a well prepared CV demonstrates the ability to organise and present information. These qualities are desirable in many jobs. Your first draft will be longer than the two pages required. You must edit the information to the required length. Only give detail on most recent or most relevant work experience. If you have sufficient work experience, just summarise your educational details.

Revise your CV on a number of occasions. Each time you should find better ways to present the information. Consider every item on your CV. Certain neutral data is required, such as your name and contact details. Every other single word should sell your suitability. Continue to refine your CV until you can no longer improve it. Check internet recruitment sites for ideas on format, content and presentation.

Double check all dates on your CV. Mistakes could leave unexplained gaps in your career. Overlapping dates will show up as an obvious error.

The finished CV should be well presented. It should be easy to read and understand. Keep the layout simple and uncluttered. Keep words, sentences and paragraphs short. Use wide margins, clear spaces and bold print. This makes it easier to scan for information.

Target your CV to the vacancy

Your CV needs to be targeted to the job requirements. In theory the same CV can be used for a number of applications. After all, it contains all the critical information that most employers require. However, sending the same standardised CV to all vacancies reduces your success rate. The company expects you to target your CV to their vacancy. If you do not, they will assume that you have sent the same standard CV to multiple vacancies. If you cannot be bothered to target your application, then you are not the sort of person they want.

A targeted CV is specific, relevant and tailored to the job requirements. Use the same keywords as the advertisement to describe your skills and experience. These are the words used by the employer to describe the essential and desirable job criteria. Edit your standard CV to only include the most relevant information. Your first edit for a particular job might stretch to the third page. Use further edits to remove whatever is not necessary.

Younger applicants

Younger applicants have less full time work experience. They must therefore include greater detail on education, qualifications, temporary or part time work experience, personal interests and hobbies. Give a short summary of:

- What you have contributed.
- What you gained from your involvement.
- How you developed valuable job related skills.

Examples include teamwork, communication skills, organising skills, leadership, etc.
Include all appropriate experience and responsibility. Include any special projects you carried out, training received and vocational courses you attended.

Highlight any transferable skills that can be applied to the advertised post. Stress any repeat work experience with the same employer. This shows that you have demonstrated your worth to an employer.

CVs from applicants with more experience

If you are a more experienced applicant, concentrate on your most recent experience. A briefer outline is sufficient for earlier jobs.

Clarify the depth and range of your experiences. Indicate your responsibilities in terms of the number of staff you supervised, budget level you managed, production output, etc. Many job titles are similar. The level of your responsibilities may not be obvious.

Include any promotions, or temporary acting up or extension to duties.

Tips on constructing your CV

- Use a confident tone and positive language.
- Summarise your responsibilities.
- Concentrate on the quality of your achievements, not the quantity.
- Quantify the savings you brought to previous employers.
- List your most relevant experience and skills on page one.
- Only include supporting information relevant to the vacancy.
- Use the same keywords used in the advertised vacancy.
- List matching skills for all of the specified essential skills
- List matching skills for as many of the desirable skills as possible.
- Limit the overall length to two pages.
- Remove all spelling and grammatical errors

Include important information on page one

Present your main selling points on the first page of your CV. You must grab the reader's attention from the outset. Include all the major reasons for inviting you to interview in the top half of page one. The remainder of your CV contains supporting information.

Keep the employer's viewpoint in mind. Make it easy to extract the relevant information. Remember that the reader only sees what you choose to include in your CV. This gives maximum scope to sell your suitability. A lot of applicants miss the opportunity to do just this.

Quantify your accomplishments

Quantify your accomplishments in terms of the benefits to your employer. Use clear metrics as in the following examples:

- Reduced annual labour costs by £150,000.
- Improved perfect quality rate from 95% to 97%.
- Reduced overheads by 10%.
- Reduced annual material waste by 15%.
- Increased annual sales by 10%.

Note these achievements are usually written in the past tense. Make sure you are consistent in the use of tense.

Focus on your personal impact

Show how your efforts benefited your employer. Use active verbs such as 'introduced,' 'implemented,' or 'initiated.' These are better than more passive terms such as 'managed,' 'maintained,' or 'supervised.'

Employers seek problem solvers, not someone who passes them on to their boss. They want someone who can cut costs, increase sales or improve performance. They value employees who overcome obstacles, speed up delivery or increase profits. The type of person who can work to deadlines and meet targets. Someone to whom they can delegate responsibility.

Double check against specified job criteria

When you have completed your CV, check that you have listed all the matching competencies. Include practical evidence for all of the specified job requirements.

The Professional CV

Many agencies produce professionally presented CVs for an agreed fee. They will send you a form to complete and return. They use this information to produce a professional CV on good quality paper. They will provide a specified number of copies. The professional CV will stand out from other applications. However recruiters will know that you did not personally prepare the CV.

The professional writer will target your CV to the particular vacancy. The problem is that it will not be targeted for the next vacancy. Purchasing a new CV each time is an expensive process. Many applicants prefer to use the professional CV service on the first occasion. They then scan or copy the CV into a word processing file and amend it for each subsequent application.

How much time will the employer spend considering my CV?

A typical job advertisement for a single vacancy could attract 500 applicants. Only about 12 candidates might be called to interview. The person reading your CV may be sifting through hundreds of similar applications. Make sure that the relevant information is accessible. If not, your CV could be discarded in less than 30 seconds.

The initial short listing may not be carried out by someone familiar with the job requirements. The immediate supervisor will be much too busy to study every application. Instead this task will be assigned to someone from the personnel department. Perhaps someone in a junior position.

The person reviewing your CV has no time to second guess your meanings or intentions. They will scan it for 20 to 30 seconds. If it doesn't look right they will discard it. So as far as you are concerned that is the end of the application process!

Matching keywords

This person sifting CVs will use a matrix with columns along the top. These will be headed with the essential and desirable job criteria. The name of each candidate will be written down the left hand side. The process involves scanning each CV and ticking off each requirement that the candidate meets. At the end of the process a given number of candidates with the most ticks will be considered for interview.

This scan includes looking for key words that match the exact job requirements as specified in the advertisement. You must use exactly the same words in your CV. This person may not recognise equivalent or similar terms for your competencies. This will lead to rejection of an acceptable application. A cluttered CV may also cause them to miss essential criteria and reject your application.

References

Never supply details of referees on your CV unless the company requests this information. The interview is the appropriate time to provide details of referees.

At the interview give the names, addresses and telephone numbers of two referees. Use previous employers who are familiar with your work. Only provide a character reference if you are requested to do so.

If you have no previous work experience, ask a teacher from your previous school, college, or university to act as referee.

Do not provide the name of your current employer as a referee. You do not want your current employer to know that you are seeking work elsewhere. Occasionally you might be asked for permission to approach your current employer in the event of a job offer being made.

Contacting referees

Always ask for permission before using someone's name as a referee. Let them know the type of work you are seeking. Provide your referees with your core competencies list. Also supply a copy of your CV and covering letter. They can refer to these when completing reference questionnaires. Remember to keep your referees informed of your progress. Thank them for their help. Use referees who are familiar with your recent work achievements. Approach someone with whom you got on well.

Ask your referee for a signed copy of the reference. This may include something with which you are not happy. If this is the case, approach someone else and repeat the process. You can include a written testimonial from a referee with your application.

Always supply a telephone number for referees. Employers prefer to telephone and speak to referees. They ask them why you left the job and whether or not they would re-employ you. A telephone reference check is quicker and saves the referee the bother of filling in forms. Your prospective new employer receives a more frank assessment of your ability and performance. Written references seldom contain negative information. Employers are hesitant to include in writing what they might divulge in a conversation.

Never include referee details on any CV you send to recruitment agencies. They may contact them before you have been interviewed and offered a job. Simply indicate that references are available on request.

Honesty is the best policy

Only include factual information in your CV. Remember you can omit anything that does not support your application. You do not want any falsehoods discovered at interview. Uncertainty over one minor item will cast doubt on the validity of the remainder of your CV. You will not be offered the position.

If you are hired and the company later finds out that information on your CV was false, your contract will be terminated.

You will be much more relaxed at the interview if you know that your CV is completely factual. If you spend the whole interview covering something up, you will not perform well. The interviewer will sense that something was not quite right about you. If he has any niggling doubts about you, he will not offer you the job. He will go with his gut feeling.

You can leave out any negative or non supporting information from your CV. For example if you failed GCSE Geography and it is not required, then omit this. Just include the exams you did pass. It is also acceptable to portray your achievements in the best light. However you cannot include blatant lies. You cannot claim better grades in exams than you achieved. Similarly never claim to have held a more senior position such as general manager when you were shift foreman. This information will eventually be unearthed and could lead to dismissal.

What not to include in your CV

Your CV needs to be clear, simple and concise. To avoid a cluttered look, only include the appropriate information. Leave out anything that is irrelevant or negative.

Do not include any of the following information in your CV:

- The title CV or Curriculum Vitae.
- Age or date of birth.
- Marital status.
- Maiden name.
- Details of children.
- Nationality.
- Work contact details.
- National insurance number.
- Religious or political affiliation.
- Gender.
- Personal details such as height and weight.
- Your medical condition.
- Previous salary details or salary aspirations.
- Reasons for leaving previous jobs.
- Non supporting information.
- Short training courses attended.
- A photograph of yourself, unless requested to do so by the firm.

- Driving license details, unless requested or applying for a driving job.
- Humour.
- References. These can be supplied later.

Common CV faults

The following list contains the most common CV faults that lead to rejection:

- Too long.
- Too cluttered.
- Spelling and grammar errors.
- Poor layout, format, design or presentation which is difficult to follow.
- Poor quality paper, print or photocopy.
- Exaggerated content.
- CV not targeted to the job requirements.
- Emphasis on responsibilities rather than achievements.
- Emphasis on qualifications rather than skills.
- Too much irrelevant detail.
- Not enough relevant supporting information.
- Emphasis on early career rather than recent experience.
- Applicant perceived to be under qualified.
- Applicant perceived to be overqualified.
- Ambiguous content.
- Unexplained gaps in dates between jobs.
- Too many extracurricular activities.
- Jargon or clichés.
- Repetition.
- Acronyms.
- No cover letter or poor cover letter.

Chapter 6. The Application Form

Many companies specify that applicants must submit an application form rather than a CV. The completed forms are used to draw up a short list of suitable candidates to invite to interview.

The application form provides employers with a standard format document. This facilitates comparisons between applicants. If a large number of applicants are expected, the company will opt to use application forms.

Companies prefer application forms because:

- They can gather all the information they need.
- Quicker screening is possible due to the standard format.
- It is easy to see if candidates have the key requirements.
- Omissions or gaps are easier to spot.
- Inconsistencies show up more readily.
- It reduces the number of respondents.

It is easy to submit a CV to multiple vacancies. Only serious candidates spend the extra time required to complete an application form.

Companies use a variety of application forms, depending on the job type or seniority level. They might use one application form for office staff and a different form for process operators.

Preparation

You need to spend a lot of time and take great care when completing an application form. The company will short list on the basis of the information you provide.

Consider the employer's viewpoint. What qualities will they deem most important? What essential and desirable criteria have they specified in the advertisement? Your application must match the specified job requirements.

Before you attempt to complete the application form:

- Read the entire document.
- Pay close attention to all instructions.
- Read any accompanying literature.
- Read the advertised vacancy again.
- Read background material on the company.
- Consider the main job requirements.
- Select your most relevant experience.

First Draft

Take a photocopy of the blank form. Fill this out first. Use your CV as a guide to help you complete the form. Before you begin get a blank sheet of paper. List the specified essential and desirable criteria. Beside each criteria list your matching skills, qualifications and experience. Make sure that each of these is included somewhere in your first draft of the completed form. Tick them off one at a time. If anything has not been included, work it in to your answer to one of the sections.

Complete the first draft. Now check the spelling, punctuation and grammar. Correct any errors. Amend anything that you do not like. Information you completed in one area might work better inserted in a different section. Summarize anything that is too long. Fit your information into the available space. This process enables you to perfect your answers. It means you do not have to make amendments on the form itself.

Have a friend check it also. They may spot additional grammar or spelling mistakes. They may suggest better ways to present the information. If you are a student, ask your career advisor to check your completed draft.

Completing the form

After you have completed the first draft leave it overnight. Read it again the next day. Make any corrections or additions as necessary. Then copy the details to the form itself.

Follow any special instructions such as:

- Completing the form in black ink.
- Listing more recent work experience first.
- Use of block capitals.
- Completing all sections of the form.
- Providing any required supporting documentation.
- Signing and dating the form.

In addition you should:

- Be as neat and tidy as possible.
- Include all the pertinent information.
- Omit irrelevant or non supporting information.
- If required, use a separate piece of A4 paper for any further details.
- Include your name at the top of any separate sheets and staple to the form.

Untidy or illegible forms may be rejected. Also essential information may be overlooked. Do not leave sections blank and refer the reader to an attached CV. The company has designed the form to standardise information from all applicants. If you cannot be bothered completing the form you will not be short listed. The employer will assume that you will take similar short cuts in the job.

There might be a section that does not refer to you. In that case write 'not applicable' in the section. For example you might be asked for work permit details when you don't need one.

Attachments

The employer may photocopy forms in the short listing process. Attached sheets often become separated at this stage. Put your name, job applied for, and reference number at the top of the attached sheets. Refer to any separate sheets in the form itself.

Sign the declaration

The application form usually contains a declaration statement at the end. You are asked to sign in order to verify the validity of the content. If you forget to sign this section your application will be rejected.

Employment history

Include employment history in reverse chronological order, unless otherwise requested.
Only include details of previous salaries if requested. You may be asked to give your reasons for leaving previous jobs. Do not include negative details about a previous employer or job. If you do you will not be short listed. Give your reasons for joining the new company. This will put a positive emphasis on your reasoning. Perhaps you wanted to gain more experience, or improve your prospects.

Flexibility

You may be asked if you are willing to work shifts or overtime. You may be asked if you are willing to travel. You will not be short listed unless you specify that you are willing to accept these requirements. If you accept the job, you should later get a chance to be transferred to a different, more suitable job. You could also apply for vacancies that are only advertised internally.

Essential Criteria

Many companies include a section for detailing essential criteria. They may ask for evidence of qualifications or experience. If you leave anything blank your application will be immediately rejected. Often this section is scanned for key words. You must use the key words from the advertisement. Give a brief indication of the scope, duration, level, accountability and depth of your experience in each case.

Additional supporting information

Most forms will include a section near the end asking for additional supporting information. You must complete this section. Use your personal statement from your CV. Explain why you want to apply for the role. Stress your suitability for the role. Show how you possess all the relevant qualifications, skills, experience and personal qualities. Match in turn all the key requirements in the job advertisement with a brief list of your competencies.

Medical Questionnaire

You must complete this section fully and honestly. You must include details of any serious illness or injury if requested. You can however point out that you are now fully recovered. You no longer require medication and do not suffer from long term effects. Many conditions such as eczema can vary in the degree of severity. If your condition is mild, note that it did not affect your previous attendance record.

Salary Details

Only include salary details in application forms if requested. Companies ask for salary details for a number of reasons. It shows the level of responsibility you held in previous roles. It also enables the company to gauge the salary package that you are likely to accept. Companies are often left with a choice between two closely matched candidates. They could opt for the person willing to accept the lower amount.

References

You will often be asked to supply reference details on an application form. These will not usually be taken up unless the company is willing to offer you the job. They may ask for a reference from your current employer. Specify that your current employer should not be contacted unless they offer you the job.

Submitting your application

Keep a photocopy of the completed form. You will need to refer to this before you attend the interview. This may be several weeks later. The form can also be used as a guide when completing other application forms.

Post your application form early enough to arrive before the closing date. If time is short you can send it special delivery. This ensures delivery the following day. It also requires the recipient to sign for the letter. Include the job reference number on the envelope. Post it, unfolded, in a white A4 size envelope. Include your letter of application and any other supporting details. Include photocopies of documents like work permits. Just note that you will bring original documents to the interview.

Main Reasons for Rejecting Application Forms

- Arrived after the closing date.
- Wrong job title, lack of reference number.
- No signature on declaration.
- Questions not answered.
- Failure to respond adequately to questions.
- Failure to follow instructions.
- Unwillingness to travel, work shifts or overtime.
- Unexplained gaps in dates.
- Poor grammar, poor spelling.
- Poor layout, poor presentation.
- Emphasis on responsibilities when the form asked for achievements.
- Lack of supporting information to substantiate claims.

Chapter 7. The covering letter

Purpose of the covering letter

Always send a covering letter along with every job application. A well written cover letter will:

- Create a professional impression.
- Summarise your key competencies.
- Indicate how these closely match the job requirements.
- Highlight your strong points.
- Improve the chances that your CV will be considered.

Content

The employer will look at your covering letter first. The content of your covering letter is just as important as that of your CV. This is your first and possibly only opportunity to sell yourself. A poor quality covering letter will lead to your application being rejected.

The reader will skim through the letter. The relevant information must be easy to access. The cover letter should contain details on:

- Position applied for including job reference number.
- Where and when you saw it advertised.
- Your contact details.
- Your key strengths.
- Your relevant skills and experience.
- Your qualifications.
- Your main achievements.
- Your reason for applying.
- What you can achieve in the position.
- A closing statement, confirming your interest and welcoming an interview.

Strengthen your case

Your cover letter should strengthen your case. You must demonstrate that you possess the essential and desirable criteria. Explain why you want the job. Highlight your main selling points.

Changing career

You may wish to change direction in your career. Your experience may not be a close match to the job requirements. In this case you must highlight all your relevant experience. Stress any compensating transferable skills. Explain your reasons for wanting to change careers.

Layout

Your covering letter should be clear and concise. It should be no longer than one side of A4. Use a standard business letter format for the layout. Words, sentences and paragraphs should be short. Use bullet points to summarise your experience.

A layout of three paragraphs works best. Paragraph one introduces yourself. Specify the vacancy and where you saw the job advertised. Paragraph two includes your relevant skills, experience and achievements. Use the keywords from the advertisement. Paragraph three gives your reason for applying. Indicate what you can contribute in the role. Conclude by confirming your interest and welcoming the next stage.

Presentation and format

- Use plain, unlined, good quality A4 paper.
- Use a good quality printer.
- Use a plain clear typeface, plain font and black ink.
- If it is difficult to read your signature, then type your name beneath it.
- Always use black ink for your signature. This will photocopy better.
- Keep a copy of your letter.
- Never send a photocopy of the letter.
- Always double check spelling and grammar.

Only submit a hand written covering letter if you are requested to do so.

Advice on writing a covering letter

When writing a covering letter:

- Address the letter to the right person.
- Target the letter to the vacancy and the company.
- Keep the tone simple, polite and enthusiastic.
- Concentrate on the needs of the company.
- Highlight your strong points.
- Include your unique selling point.
- Use the same keywords as the job advertisement.
- Sign the letter.

The covering letter should be more personal than your CV. Show enthusiasm when describing the prospects of doing the job.

Avoid the following in cover letters

- Jargon or clichés.
- Repetition of words or phrases.
- Mentioning that you are currently unemployed.
- Admitting that you lack qualifications or experience.
- Aspirations of better salary or conditions.
- Surplus detail.
- Spelling or grammar mistakes.

Chapter 8. The speculative application

Speculative applications are sent to companies who have not advertised a vacancy. The theory being that a position might come up soon. The applicants hope that their initiative might get them an interview.

The speculative letter aims to access the invisible job market. This is where vacancies exist, but are not yet advertised. If you apply at the right time you might be invited to attend an interview. The advantage you gain is that there will be few other candidates. The advantage to the company is that it saves on advertising and short listing costs.

If there are no current vacancies the company may retain your application on file for a specified period.

Target the right companies

Speculative applications can be a waste of time and effort. Many companies do not bother to reply to them. You need to target your efforts. Apply to companies where suitable vacancies are likely to arise in the short term. Larger firms tend to have more vacancies. Local papers include articles on companies relocating to or expanding in a particular area.

Target the right job

Work out what kind of job is likely to be available. Prepare your CV accordingly. Outline the type of job you want in the covering letter. Do not to be too specific in your requirements. This will reduce your chances of being considered. Indicate that you can be flexible in the type of work you can undertake. Describe your work related and personal skills. Note that you will follow up with a phone call the following week.

Target the right person

You also need to send the application to the correct person. Never send a speculative letter to the personnel department. They will not process it if they do not have an advertised vacancy. Send your application to the immediate boss of the position you are seeking. Ring the company up and get his details before submitting your application.

The speculative letter needs to be unique. If it is not targeted to the company, the job and the right person, it will be discarded.

Chapter 9. On-line applications

The internet has become the favoured medium in the recruitment process. Many firms advertise vacancies on their own websites. Recruitment agencies host on-line recruitment websites. University career organisations have on-line job boards. There are also dedicated employment websites. Government and local agencies host career based websites.

Advantages to the employer

Companies advertise jobs on-line for a number of reasons:

- Recruitment costs are lower.
- Jobs can be advertised more efficiently.
- A larger audience can be targeted.
- Applications can be processed more efficiently.
- Advertisements are available to viewers until the posting is removed.
- The method can be combined with automated selection tests.

Automated processing of on-line applications

Larger firms use systems that can automatically filter on-line applications. Completed applications are compared with predetermined job criteria using key word searches. Some systems provide a scoring mechanism. The benefits are a more efficient recruitment and selection process. The downside is higher initial costs of hardware and software design.

Advantages to the applicant

On-line applications provide the following advantages:

- A simple, quicker, more efficient process.
- You can gain access to a greater number and variety of vacancies.
- Reduced costs. There is no need for printing costs, stationery, stamps and envelopes.

- Information on company websites is easy to access and regularly updated.
- You will not be rejected for trivial reasons, such as forgetting to sign forms, poor handwriting, etc.
- You can sometimes simply click to attach your CV.
- You can make your CV available to many employers at the same time.
- You can update your CV on-line.

Completing on-line application forms

Take great care when completing on-line applications. Print out the form in advance. Study it carefully. Fill it out by hand. Follow the advice included in chapter 6 on completing application forms. Make sure you are satisfied with this completed hard copy. Then copy the details to the on-line application.

Take your time when keying in the information. It is easy to make typing errors. Often you will not realise that you have done so. Copy and paste each completed section into a word processing file. You can then check the spelling and grammar.

Allow yourself plenty of time to complete the application. Make use of any facility to save the form and return to it. This avoids rushing the process. It is sometimes easier to discover mistakes when you return to the work.

When you have finished, keep a printed copy of your on-line application. You will need this for future reference.

On-line CVs

When submitting your on-line CV:

- Keep content clear and concise.
- Use simple formats and plain fonts.
- Use the identical keywords as used in the job advertisement.
- Include all contact details at the top.

Do not send the same CV to all on-line vacancies. Send targeted, job specific, applications to each vacancy. Retain a printed copy of your on-line CV for later reference.

CV Databases

Job sites and job boards create on-line CV databases of job seekers. CV databases may be general or specialised. Potential employers key in their requirements such as job title, industry sector, salary and location. The CV database search engine then provides a list of matching CVs. This is usually minus the contact details. The employer may find some suitable matches. They can then access the contact details for an agreed fee.

Electronic scanning of CVs

Some firms will scan your printed CV. They use software to search for keywords. The results will determine if your CV is accepted or rejected. This is why you must use exactly the same competency keywords as used in the job advertisement.

Double check all spelling. Typing errors and irregular fonts may not be interpreted correctly. This could lead to rejection of your CV.

Security

Consider the security of your data when using on-line recruitment agencies or CV databases. Make sure that any agency you use complies with the Recruitment and Employment Confederation Code of Practice.

Chapter 10. Selection tests

Larger companies regularly use selection tests as part of their recruitment process. Tests are designed to measure specific job related skills. Test results are used to predict job performance. Pass levels are set at a level required to do the job competently. If you fail the test it is assumed that you lack the specified job related skills.

Advantages to the company

Companies favour selection tests because:

- Tests are cost effective.
- Tests can be tailored to a particular job.
- Many applicants can be tested at the same time.
- Tests reduce subjectivity in the selection process.
- Their use ensures a fairer selection process.
- Tests are independent.
- Their use protects the company against claims of discrimination.
- Tests can measure current ability and predict future performance.
- The results can be combined with other short listing methods.
- Tests can be marked automatically by computers.
- Personality profiles can be generated from test results.

Advantage to the applicants

Some candidates do not perform well at interviews. They may be nervous or self-conscious. Their test score gives the interviewer a more objective view of their performance.

Criteria for selection tests

Properly designed tests should be:

- Relevant, by measuring criteria specific to the job.
- Objective and fair to all candidates.
- Standardised, with all applicants sitting the same tests.

- Reliable in producing consistent results.
- Valid in measuring what they purport to measure.

The test must discriminate fairly between those possessing the desired criteria and those lacking it. The test should not be skewed against any particular ethnic culture or group.

Tests are used in conjunction with other selection processes such as interviews or group exercises.

Types of tests

The following types of tests are commonly used:

- Ability tests.
- Aptitude tests.
- Attainment tests.
- Personality tests.
- Professional or University entrance tests.

Aptitude or ability tests can be used before the interview stage to filter out unsuitable candidates. Tests results can also be used at the end of the selection process, to provide supporting information.

Ability tests

Ability tests measure an individual's potential. They indicate the ability to acquire new skills and to learn new tasks. There are several different types of tests:

- Verbal reasoning.
- Numerical reasoning.
- Abstract reasoning.
- Spatial ability.
- IQ levels.

Verbal reasoning tests

Verbal reasoning tests are used to test language comprehension skills including vocabulary, spelling, punctuation and grammar.

Numerical reasoning tests

Numerical reasoning tests are used to test basic mental arithmetic. This includes addition, subtraction, multiplication and division. They also test the understanding and manipulation of percentages, decimals, fractions, numerical patterns and sequences.

Intelligence or IQ tests

Intelligence tests are used to measure a person's mental capacity. The results indicate learning ability. Intelligence tests are used for basic skill level jobs. They are used to eliminate applicants whose intelligence is too low, or perhaps too high. IQ tests contain spacial and diagrammatic reasoning tests.

Intelligence tests are not used for professional positions. Candidates have already obtained university degrees or professional exams. They are thus deemed to have the necessary intelligence to do the job.

Aptitude tests

Aptitude tests are designed to measure job specific skills. They measure a candidate's potential ability, after training, to do a job. The candidate must carry out certain job related tasks under controlled conditions.

There are a number of different categories of aptitude tests:

- Mechanical comprehension.
- Data checking.
- Work sample tests.

Attainment tests

Attainment tests measure skills that have already been acquired. They are based on retrospective knowledge. They do not measure potential.

These tests emulate the tasks carried out at work. Examples might be typing tests, shorthand tests or data processing. Candidates are required to check information and carry out the given task in a limited time. Accuracy is critical in this type of test.

Personality tests

Personality tests measure specific behavioural aspects required to carry out the job. They identify a person's pre-disposition to behave in a certain manner, under given conditions. Applicants must identify personal choices, preferences and values from a selection of options. The tests are designed by occupational psychologists. The aim is to identify candidates with the correct values for the job.

There is usually no time limit on personality tests. The format is usually multiple choice. Candidates are presented with hypothetical situations. They are then asked to select the most appropriate response for them.

Advice on answering personality tests

You do not need to practise for a personality test. There are no right or wrong answers to the questions. For each question go with your gut reaction and give the answer that you feel is most appropriate.

The main problem with personality tests is that candidates often give the answers they think will get them short listed for the job. This would invalidate the test results. This is why personality tests contain in-built checks and balances. The aim is to detect inconsistency in responses. You will be required to answer the same topic in several different ways throughout the test.

The test is designed to select individuals with the right personality for the job. You should not cheat the answers. You could end up in a job for which you are not suited.

However you should avoid answering questions in a manner that might suggest:

- Inability to cope with stress.
- Prejudice.
- Problems with authority.
- Disregard for rules and regulations.
- Problems with bureaucracy.
- Time keeping or attendance issues.
- Dishonesty.
- Emotional immaturity or instability.
- Relationship issues.
- Inflexibility.
- Low self-esteem.
- Turning a blind eye to rule bending by others.
- Drug dependence or abuse.

Reasoning behind personality tests

Personality tests are used to measure:

- Level of extroversion or introversion.
- Decision making ability.
- Communication skills.
- Attitude to risk taking.
- Emotional stability.
- Assertiveness level.
- Level of self-confidence.
- Flexibility.
- Tendency to conform to rules and regulations.
- Certain management skills.
- Motivation levels.
- Team working skills.

Personality tests are used as a supporting tool in the selection process. The results are not interpreted in isolation. They are backed up by an interview. The results may only be considered when final selection decisions are being made.

Integrity tests.

Integrity tests rate honesty, integrity, responsibility and reliability. The test may be incorporated within an overall personality test. Integrity tests are used for positions where the employee is likely to handle money, merchandise, customer details or trade secrets.

UKCAT and BMAT

The UKCAT or United Kingdom Clinical Aptitude Test can be taken from July to October each year by students wishing to apply to medical school. The test covers aptitude and ability. The tests are based on numerical, verbal and abstract reasoning and decision analysis. Candidates can score from 300 to 900 in each of the four tests. Performance in the test along with other application criteria determines who will be invited to interview for medical school.

The higher your UKCAT score, the more marks you earn towards the eventual admission decision. Carrying out practice tests in advance will improve a candidate's performance in the actual UKCAT test.

Some medical schools like Oxford and Cambridge require candidates to sit a similar test known as the BMAT the BioMedical Admissions Test. The BMAT also tests scientific knowledge and incorporates a written test. There are two other variants of test. Students wishing to apply to medical school should first check which tests apply to their preferred university.

Supervision of tests

Tests need to be supervised by qualified personnel. Supervisor training is carried out by the test provider. To ensure that tests are fair, consistent and reliable they must be taken under standardised conditions. Each candidate should:

- Work to the same time constraints.
- Receive the same verbal and written instructions.
- Have the same opportunity for practice.

This applies regardless of when they sit the test. Only qualified personnel should mark tests and analyse results.

Preparing for tests

Ability and aptitude tests usually have right or wrong answers. The test must be completed in a limited time slot. Applicants must answer as many questions as possible. The format is usually multiple choice questions. Most people will have encountered these types of tests at school.

You can improve your score by obtaining and completing practice tests in advance. This will help to familiarise you with the types of question. Your answering technique will improve. The more you practise the better you will perform in the real test. This will also boost your confidence.

Ring the personnel department if you are asked to take part in a selection test. Find out which type of test they will be using. Practice tests are available at most good book shops or on-line at some recruitment sites. Specialised books offer invaluable advice and practice.

The day of the test

Make sure you get a good night's sleep in advance. Turn up for the test in good time. Group tests will begin on time. You will not be admitted if you are late. This would disrupt other candidates. Inform the employer in advance if you have a disability requiring special arrangements. Remember to bring any reading glasses. Bring a watch to check your progress.

Advice on taking tests

- Listen carefully to all verbal instructions prior to the test.
- Do exactly as instructed.
- Read all written instructions carefully.
- If time is available, read all instructions twice.
- Ask for any necessary clarification before the test begins.
- Don't assume anything.
- Work out, in advance, the available time to answer each question.
- Find out if calculators are permitted.
- Work through the examples provided.
- Record your answers exactly as you are instructed.
- Regularly check that your answers are recorded in the correct section.
- Make sure any alterations are clear.
- Work as quickly and accurately as possible.
- Answer as many questions as possible.
- Monitor your time as you progress.
- Do not dwell too long on any one question.
- If experiencing difficulties, skip to the next question.
- If unsure about an answer, have a guess.
- Finish the test before going back to check your answers.
- If you finish early and have skipped some questions, tackle them first.

Tests are designed so that most people will not complete all the questions. Tests may become progressively more difficult as you proceed through them. Your must complete as many questions correctly in the limited time available. Your score is rated against the performance of a control group of past applicants.

Find out in advance if you lose marks for wrong answers. If not, you can guess. Sometimes in multiple choice questions you can eliminate say, three of five possible answers as being definitely wrong. You now have a one in two chance of guessing correctly, rather than one in five.

Storage of test results

Many companies keep tests results for up to two years. Tests results should be treated as confidential. They should have restricted access. They should not be stored in open ended databases. The storage and retention of results is subject to The Data Protection Act 1998.

Chapter 11. Preparing for the interview

You must be able to convince the interviewer that you are the best person for the job. To do this you must prepare in advance. Gather all the required evidence to make your case for selection. What makes you the best choice? What is your unique selling point?

The goal of your interview preparation should be to help you:

- Overcome the interviewer's objections.
- Meet the interviewer's expectations.
- Show how you are the best match for the job requirements.

The Letter of Invitation

Do not feel apprehensive if you are invited to an interview. Receiving an invite is a positive sign. It indicates that the employer believes from your application that you can do the job. The vast majority of candidates will already have been rejected during the short listing stage. Most will lack the minimum requirements to do the job. Others will have been rejected for submitting poor quality applications.

You now have a great chance of securing the job offer. You just need to carry out the proper preparation and research. Respond and confirm your attendance if this has been requested in the letter of invitation.

The need for proper preparation

Proper preparation is essential if you want to secure a job offer. Many applicants only carry out enough research to complete the application form. They have little or no chance of securing a job offer.

Such applicants might look a great prospect on paper. However, it is obvious at interview that they have not considered their suitability. They have not anticipated the likely questions. They have not worked out how to present their case. Employers assume that such candidates are not interested in the job. The company will offer the job to someone who has shown greater interest in and enthusiasm for the role.

Do not overlook your preparation if you want the job. Without adequate preparation you will not succeed at the interview stage. Remember the adage "Fail to prepare then prepare to fail." Begin your preparation the moment you have decided to apply. Continue with it until you arrive at the interview room.

Prepare early

A certain amount of preparation is required to complete the application form. This will have involved matching your competencies with the essential and desirable job requirements. Having sent off your application, you need to continue your preparation.

Use the time wisely between sending off your application and receiving an invite to interview. This may take several weeks. Your scheduled interview date may only be a few days after you receive the invite letter.

Building an application folder

Build a folder containing your interview preparation notes. This keeps all the relevant information in one place. You can refer to this file at each stage of the process. Keep the following information in the folder:

- Job advertisement.
- Interview details – date, time, type, interviewer names and positions.
- Job description.
- Person specification.
- Company information.
- Your letter of application.
- Your CV or application form.

- Any correspondence with the firm.
- Your matching job related skills.
- Your personal matching competency list.
- The questions you anticipate being asked.
- Your prepared answers to anticipated questions.
- Your written questions for the interviewer.
- Your post interview analysis.

It is important to keep these details. Your application form or CV will be specific to this particular vacancy. You will need to study the file before attending the interview.
Create a different application folder for each separate application you make.

Consider the employer's needs

The interview questions will be based on the job requirements and your CV or application form. You should be able to talk about any information you have provided.

Think about the employer's perspective. What kind of employee do they want? The essential and desirable selection criteria will be outlined in the advertisement. Further details are available in the job description and the person specification. Do you possess all the essential criteria? If not, have you got any equivalent qualifications or experiences? You must stress these if you wish to be short listed. Do you have any of the desirable criteria? List examples from your own experiences.

Consider how the job integrates with others

Where does the job fit into the organisation? How will the job holder interact within the department? Will he work alone or as part of a team? What kind of interpersonal skills are required? These factors will help determine the likely questions. It will also influence your answers.

Think about how the job integrates with the rest of the organisation. Will you have internal suppliers and customers? Will you be in regular contact with other parts of the organisation? What will their needs be? How will you be expected to interact with these other areas? What knowledge and skills will be required?

Think about the nature of the job. Consider the initiative required, leadership skills, creativity, problem solving or other demands.

Consider how the job matches your career goals

Is this job a logical step in your career path? Will it add to your skill set? Will it broaden your experience? Will it help you get to where you eventually want to be?

Think about how your career has developed over the years. Have you followed a consistent path? Has there been a common thread in your job choices? Why have you changed direction at particular times during your career? What are your immediate and longer term career plans? What is your future potential? Be prepared to talk about these issues.

Prepare a competency list of practical accomplishments

Prepare a competency list based on your main accomplishments. List some practical examples from your work experience. This should be in the format of:

- The problems you encountered.
- The options you considered.
- The corrective actions you took.
- The quantifiable benefits that accrued to your employer.
- What you learned from the experience.
- How this experience can benefit your new employer.

Summarise these to a few paragraphs in each case. List one or two examples for each of the categories included in Chapter 14. These are the main competencies in which you will be scored. They fall under the broad sectors of competence, commitment to the job, and compatibility.

With every incident you describe, indicate how you:

- Remained positive and tackled the problem with enthusiasm.
- Considered the consequences to other personnel and departments.
- Were aware of your own limitations.
- Asked for assistance if you needed it from others or your boss.
- Came to a compromise where necessary.
- Took positive action to avoid any potential conflict.
- Reviewed your actions to consider how you could have handled things better.

People find it easy to remember short stories or narratives. Interviewers recall these stories. They tend to forget simple claims that you possess certain desirable personal characteristics.

Use you competency list to expand on your CV

Your competency list should be in addition to any information contained in your CV. Use this list to help answer competency based questions throughout the interview. Give each example where you feel it is most appropriate.

Demonstrate that you will fit in

Proper research on the company and the job helps you show how you will settle in the role. It enables you demonstrate how you can contribute to the team. This is one of the three main selection criteria.

Give evidence of your work ethic

You must convince the interviewer that you have worked hard in previous roles. This is the best indicator that you will apply yourself to any new role. He will look for signs that you have persevered, overcome problems and got results. This is why he will ask about subjects you disliked at school and duties you found difficult at work. Every job has difficult chores. You will not find all aspects of the job appealing. However you must work hard at all tasks, in order to get the job done.

Find out which type of interview you will be attending

Find out in advance which type of interview you will be attending. Is it a screening interview or a selection interview? Your approach will differ depending on the type of interview as explained in Chapter 15.

Find out who will be carrying out the interview

Ring up in advance and speak to someone from the personnel department. Find out the format and likely duration of the interview. Find out the names and roles of the interviewers. Look them up on the company website. Find out their current and previous roles. This will help you anticipate the types of questions they are likely to ask. It will give you a head start in building rapport at interview.

Chapter 12. The interviewer's perspective

Understand what the employer wants

In order to secure a job offer you must first appreciate things from the interviewer's perspective. You must understand:

- The qualities he finds desirable.
- The qualities that he is looking to avoid.
- The methods he employs to detect and eliminate unsuitable candidates.

The risk factor

Selecting employees is a risky business. There is no guaranteed methodology. Attracting the right calibre of employees is vital to the long term success of a business.

However it is not easy to select the best candidate for a job. The process is prone to error. The interviewer is attempting to assess each candidate's personality and suitability on the basis of a short interview.

The interviewer can be as anxious and concerned about the process as the candidate. Getting the decision wrong leads to undesirable repercussions, in the short to medium term. This will cause his judgement to be questioned. If he repeatedly gets the decision wrong it will affect his credibility.

Hiring the wrong person can cost over double the annual salary of that employee by the time the situation is rectified. These costs consist of:

-Internal management's costs assessing the reasons behind the poor selection.
- Any alterations required to the interview questions or scoring system.
- Management costs reviewing the exit strategy for the unsuccessful appointee.

- Redundancy costs for the initial appointee.
- Wasted induction and training costs.
- Disruption to the rest of the team.
- Impact on productivity and morale.
- Re-advertising costs.
- Re-interviewing costs.
- Reluctance of future candidates to take the position if the last person only stayed a few months.

The biggest single factor leading to staff turnover is the inability of new employees to fit in with the company culture. This is why employers are anxious to get the decision right. Unhappy employees are often disruptive and eventually leave. Think about how you can alleviate the interviewer's concerns about your suitability.

The interviewer's preparation

An experienced interviewer will evaluate the job. He will then list the preconditions for an ideal candidate. He will rank these requirements in order of relevance and importance. He will prepare a list of questions to ask each candidate. He will consult with the immediate supervisor for the vacant position. He will enlist this person onto the interview panel at the selection interview stage. The immediate supervisor must make the ultimate selection decision. The two should arrive at an agreed choice free from personal bias.

The interviewer will be concerned about the danger of hiring the best performing interviewee. This may not necessarily be the most suitable candidate for the job itself.

The difficulties confronting the interviewer

A myriad of problems confront the interviewer as the interview progresses. From the outset he must work to a tight schedule within a rigid framework. To compound his problems most candidates will begin in an apprehensive, self-conscious and defensive manner. Nervous interviewees are more hesitant, communicate less and divulge little about themselves.

To make matters worse each candidate will portray himself in the most favourable light. In normal circumstances people have a natural tendency to overestimate their talents and underestimate their faults. Put them in an interview situation and this tendency will be magnified. Candidates will conceal weaknesses and exaggerate strengths. This is why the interviewer will scrutinises body language. He will attempt to get past any façade. He will try to uncover the real personality hidden behind the mask.

Any fair assessment of candidates is extremely difficult under such trying circumstances.

Fair Employment Legislation

It is illegal for employers to discriminate in terms of sex, colour, race, ethnicity, national origin, or religious denomination. A lot of employment legislation has been introduced to enforce the rights of employees. Some examples include:

Equal Pay Act 1970 – stated that pay and contracts should be equal for men and women doing like work.
Sex Discrimination Act 1975 – made it unlawful to discriminate directly or indirectly on the grounds of sex, gender reassignment or marital status. Employees can take their case to an employment tribunal.
Race Relations Act 1976 – made it unlawful to treat individuals less favourably on the grounds of colour, race, ethnic origin or nationality.
Fair Employment Act (NI) 1989. - made it unlawful to discriminate on the basis of religious beliefs.
Disability Discrimination Act 1995 – made it unlawful to discriminate directly or indirectly against disabled people. Employers must make reasonable adjustments to accommodate a disabled person's needs.
Equality Act 2006 – established The Commission for Equality.

These acts cover every stage of the selection process. They also cover the training, promotion and discipline of employees.

Statutory bodies provide employers with recruitment guidelines and codes of practice. The Commission for Racial Equality and The Equal Opportunities Commission are two such bodies. In addition the Institute of Personnel Management also provide member companies in the UK and the Republic of Ireland with a recruitment code.

Every company must be aware of the latest recruitment legislation, guidelines and codes of practice. They must follow the procedures as outlined by the relevant statutory bodies.

Following the guidelines in practice

Employers must treat all candidates in the same manner. The interview and any tests must be structured in the same way for all applicants. Each candidate must be given an equal chance to make their case for selection. The interviewer will try to be fair, unbiased and impartial with all candidates. During the interview he should:

- Ensure that there will be no interruptions by visitors or phone calls.
- Put each candidate at ease from the start.
- Start by outlining the process, the time scale and the key areas to be covered.
- Establish and maintain rapport with each candidate.
- Allow the interviewee to talk for about 70% of the time.
- Use a friendly, informal and unassuming approach.
- Begin with simple, non contentious issues and questions.
- Allow the candidate time to consider his response before answering.
- Let the candidate settle down before asking more demanding questions.
- Ask each candidate the same core questions.
- Keep questions short and clear.
- Use open ended questions.
- Pay attention to how each candidate answers the questions.

- Show interest and encourage each candidate to fully express themselves.
- Use supportive gestures such as nodding and smiling to promote responses.
- Avoid using loaded, trick or leading questions.
- Avoid using argumentative or aggressive tactics.
- Take notes discreetly, so as not to unsettle the candidates.
- Keep the interview on track and to schedule.
- Avoid interrupting the candidate.
- Remain impartial and avoid personal bias and prejudice.
- Avoid jumping to conclusions.
- Keep an open mind throughout.
- Encourage all candidates to ask questions.
- Leave final selection decisions until after everyone has been interviewed.
- At the end of the interview, let the candidate know what the next stage will be.

The interviewer must get the candidate to open up and reveal extra information. It is in the interviewer's interest to build and maintain rapport. He uses this rapport to probe areas of significant interest or concern. He will concentrate on more recent and relevant experience. He will ignore earlier, less relevant, experience so as not to disconcert the candidate.

Methods of assessing candidates

Employers usually design their own scoring sheets. They use these to assess the suitability of each candidate. However they must adhere to fair employment legislation. Many larger firms have an equal opportunities policy. Employers will follow the acknowledged standards and guidelines for selection procedures.

The assessment method should be flexible enough to cover a wide variety of jobs. However assessment sheets may vary depending on the nature and level of the particular job. Candidates receive marks for job related skills and experience. They are also assessed on key personal attributes that are deemed desirable.

The scoring sheet provides a structured framework to facilitate comparison between candidates. It also helps to keep the interview on track.

Chapter 13. Reasons for rejecting candidates

The interviewer's major concerns.

The interviewer wants to avoid hiring anyone who:

- Cannot do the job.
- Needs a lot of initial training and supervision.
- Has little self-motivation and drive.
- Will not work hard.
- Will contribute as little as possible.
- Will miss targets and deadlines.
- Will have problems with authority.
- Will not accept criticism.
- Will not perform as a team member.
- Will engage in office politics.
- Will not settle in the role.
- Will disturb others.
- Will have attendance problems.
- Will leave as soon as they get a better offer elsewhere.
- Will undermine his judgement for selecting such a poor employee.

Weeding out unsuitable candidates

Many interviewers find it easier to eliminate unsuitable candidates than to make the final recruitment decision. Screening interviews are designed to weed out everyone except the select few best qualified applicants. Interviewers place much more emphasis on negative characteristics than on positive traits. In this way they reduce the list down to a few probable prospects. The hope being, that one of the remaining candidates will suit the role. This is why you must never reveal any negative information about yourself.

Common reasons why candidates are not offered the job.

- Arriving late for interview.

- Poor personal appearance.
- Poor body language or lack of eye contact.
- Problems conforming to authority.
- Being negative about previous employers.
- Difficulties working with colleagues in their previous roles.
- Inadequate research on the company and the job requirements.
- Being unfamiliar with the contents of their CV, or application form.
- Not presenting additional information beyond their CV contents.
- Not linking their experience to the job requirements.
- Not producing evidence of their achievements.
- Not emphasising transferable skills.
- Wrong skill set for the job
- Not rating the vacancy as their first choice.
- Having no clear idea why they want the job.
- No clear career goals.
- Blaming others for their shortcomings.
- Conceited, aggressive or superior attitude.
- Lack of courtesy.
- Poor communication or presentation skills.
- Unrealistic ambition.
- Signs of dishonesty, deceit, concealment or evasive behaviour.
- Lack of self-motivation and commitment.
- Lack of enthusiasm or indifference.
- Lack of maturity.
- Anxiety and nerves.
- Self-doubt and poor self-esteem.
- Procrastination or difficulties making decisions.
- Revealing too many weaknesses.
- Under qualified.
- Overqualified.
- Talking too much.
- Lack of tact.
- Concentrating on their own needs and interests, instead of those of the firm.
- Over exaggerating skills or experiences.
- Inability to deal with criticism.
- Having no questions, or asking poor questions.
- Poor time keeping and attendance.

- Unrealistic salary expectations.
- Inflexibility on working patterns, overtime, job location or travel.

If you want to avoid being rejected for the position, you must avoid all of these common pitfalls. You must be enthusiastic about taking up the role.

Do not speak negatively about others

Anyone displaying problems with authority or work colleagues will be deemed as potentially disruptive. No one wants to hire a complainer with a negative outlook. Such employees resist change and throw up obstacles to progress. Only divulge positive information about your relationships in previous roles.

Convince the employer that the job is your first choice

If you do not convince the interviewer that the vacancy is your first choice you will not receive an offer. It's OK to say that you are applying for other jobs, but they need to be related. You must, however, stress that this job is your first choice. Give reasons for this.

Be confident in your abilities

Companies expect new appointees to settle in and make worthwhile contributions much quicker than in the past. This is because employees do not remain with companies as long as they did historically. You are expected to make an impact much faster. You therefore need to possess self-confidence. You must have the ability and willingness to learn new tasks. If the interviewer suspects that you doubt your ability to undertake the job, you will not be short listed for the position.

Be realistic in your expectations

The interviewer will be cautious of any sign of unrealistic ambition. Appointees who fail to settle into a new job are often overambitious, or have a past history of hopping from one job to another. The selection process is expensive and time consuming. The company does not want to repeat it unnecessarily. If you fall into any of these categories, it will be assumed that you will leave for the first improved offer. You must relay the interviewer's fears. You must convince him that you will remain in the post if appointed.

Pitch your sale to the level of the job

Your skills and qualifications must equate approximately to the job requirements. If you are under qualified you are likely to struggle. You will not be able to perform to an acceptable level. It will take too long and cost too much to bring you up to an acceptable standard.

Candidates who are overqualified tend to be bored. They lack interest and are disruptive to colleagues. They often leave for a better position elsewhere.

Be consistent

References are rarely unsatisfactory. This leaves the interviewer with only your assurance of past performance. This is why he will interrogate you closely and expect a consistent pattern of reply. Any discrepancies or anomalies may cause him to be suspicious. This will cause him to delve deeper and ask more pertinent questions. Any hints of dishonesty, deceit or concealment will lead to rejection. This includes non verbal cues, including facial expressions and body language.

Be honest

If the interviewer is obviously suspicious, do not continue to conceal some minor issue. It is already too late. He is already concerned about something. Own up and give a reasonable explanation. You can always attempt to balance the fault with a positive strength. Do not continue to be evasive. The interviewer will assume that you are hiding something more substantial.

Be selective in what you reveal

The interview should be like a presentation. You are in control of the editing process. You need to present all the best bits. If the interviewer is presented with only positive aspects of your personality, he will form a positive image of you.

The interviewers can only go on the information that you choose to reveal about yourself. They can only see 10% of the picture in terms of your personality. The interviewer will draw conclusions from this limited view. He will fill in the blanks. If there is any negative content this will be magnified. If he discovers one or two negative issues, he will assume that there is more that he has not unearthed. You will not receive a job offer.

Chapter 14. The interviewer's selection criteria

The ideal candidate

The company will draw up the profile of an ideal candidate. It is relatively easy to reject unsuitable candidates. It is much more difficult to make the final choice. The company will choose the candidate who most closely matches the profile of the ideal candidate.

The ideal candidate is:

- A team player.
- Hard working, dedicated, motivated and committed.
- A problem solver who shows initiative.
- Capable of fitting in with the company culture, policy and regulations.
- Happy and comfortable in the position.
- Optimistic and willing to embrace change.

A second interview stage may be required to facilitate the final selection decision. If you are invited to a second interview it is already accepted that you can do the job. Concentrate on showing how you will work hard, achieve results and fit in well with the existing team.

The three essential selection criteria

The hiring decision will hinge on how you are rated on certain core competencies.
Interviewers use three critical selection criteria to assess candidates:

Competence - Can the candidate do the job with minimum supervision? Will it be easy to train him?
Commitment - Will the candidate work hard in the job? Will he overcome obstacles and setbacks and achieve results?

Compatibility - Will the candidate fit in with the existing team?

In the final analysis, every interview question is asked in order to receive an answer to one of these three critical selection criteria.

Assessment of competence

The interviewer will assess your ability to do the job to the required standard. He will ask questions to help gauge the level of your core competencies. He will match these with the job requirements. He will place greater emphasis on your most recent experience. He will ask about your successes, your difficulties and your achievements.

Candidates are assessed on their job related skills and experience. The interviewer might score candidates on the following factors:

- Qualifications.
- Job related skills.
- Relevant experience.
- Supervisory experience.
- Achievements.
- Future potential.

To score well in this section you must convince the interviewer that you can do the job to a high standard.

Demonstrate your net worth to the company

Employers value employees who can achieve results that influence the bottom line. Do not just outline your experiences and responsibilities. Stress your achievements. Give examples of where you have:

-Reduced costs.
- Improved efficiencies.
- Improved productivity.
- Saved time.
- Reduced downtime.

- Increased sales.
- Improved quality.
- Improved safety standards.
- Improved customer service levels.
- Reduced waste.
- Otherwise saved the company money.

Quantify the savings you achieved. The interviewer wants to hire someone who will become a net asset. Someone who adds more worth to the company than the total cost of employing them. The interviewer will reject anyone deemed to be a liability. The type of person who add costs to the organisation without bringing any benefits to the employer.

Never assume that the interviewer understands the relevance of your experience and qualifications. Spell out exactly the benefits you can bring to the firm. Use actual examples from your past achievements.

Assessment of commitment

Work related skills indicate your ability to do the job. This is not enough to get you hired. The interviewer also scores each applicant on key personal skills related to their level of commitment. These skills indicate the propensity to perform to a high level. The results answer the interviewer's second basic question. Will you work hard and achieve results?

The interviewer will assess your level of motivation. How well have you applied yourself, both at work and at leisure activities? Anyone working hard in the past is likely to continue to do so in the future. A motivated employee should perform well in any new role, if offered the job.

The interviewer is interested in your achievements. He is less interested in roles, duties and responsibilities. He will not be swayed by unsubstantiated promises of future success. You must provide specific examples of the benefits have you brought to previous employers.

Certain fundamental skills are required in every job. Employers look for evidence of the following key personal traits:

Initiative. Self-motivation, independence and ability to make decisions. Tendency to propose new ideas and new ways of tackling problems. Continually seeking better ways to do things and get results.

Drive and determination. Following through on priorities. Ability to overcome obstacles and recover from setbacks. Eagerness to complete tasks. Goal orientated. Looking for new challenges and embracing change. Possessing energy, stamina, tenacity and resilience. Willing to work hard.

Commitment and dedication. A strong work ethic. Motivated and enthusiastic. Commitment to company goals, culture and beliefs. Willing to place organisational requirements before personal needs. Positive, resolute approach to tackling problems. A professional approach.

Flexibility. Willing to adapt to changing commercial demands. Open to change or new ideas. Willing to assist work colleagues. Willing to work overtime if requested.

Willingness to learn. Intelligence. Ability to acquire new skills and work with minimal supervision. Keen to improve knowledge and skill set.

Dependability or reliability. Punctuality. Good attendance. Willing to take on responsibility as required. Consistency of approach. Trustworthy, loyal, honest, stable, predictable and dependable nature.

Integrity. Honest approach, taking decisions based on the interests of the company. Showing interest in work. Taking care and paying attention to detail. Taking responsibility for own actions.

Problem solving and analytic skills. Rational approach to analysing problems. Able to gather data, evaluate options, apply logical thinking, formulate and test alternative solutions. Ability to decide on the optimum course of action, implement change and return quantifiable benefit. Breaking complex problems down into their constituent sectors.

Planning and organizing. Systematic approach to setting goals, prioritising tasks, scheduling workloads, coordinating action and managing projects. Reviewing progress regularly. Organizing events. Project work.

Confidence. Self-belief, self-assurance, self-reliance. Emotional stability. Trust in your own abilities. Ability to work unaided. Calmness under pressure.

Commercial awareness. Understanding how your actions affect the bottom line. Looking for ways to save money and add value. Aware of the need for economy, efficiency, productivity and innovation. Aware of the need to follow policies and procedures. Awareness of how decisions affect customers, suppliers and competitors.

Accomplishments. Achievements in education, work and leisure activities. Qualifications, exam results, training, awards. Benefits you have brought to your employer. Cost savings and reduction of waste. Improvements in efficiency, productivity, sales, quality and safety.

Circumstance. There may be special circumstances required such as working unsocial shifts, the need to travel or flexibility in work hours.

Younger candidates are not disadvantaged when compared with their older counterparts. The interviewer takes into account age and circumstances.

Assessment of compatibility

The interviewer wants to know if you will be compatible. This is the third basic question that he needs answered. Will you fit in well and contribute to the existing team?

The interviewer will look for someone with the following interpersonal skills:

Disposition. Acceptable appearance, character, personality, temperament, nature.

Teamwork. Ability to work confidently within a group. Willing to resolve conflict or difficulties. Displaying tact and diplomacy. Putting the needs of the team above personal desires. Getting the most from others. Possessing good interpersonal skills. Building and maintaining relationships. Enabling, facilitating, liaising, supporting, helping, consulting, and listening.

Leadership skills. Having the ability to motivate and direct others. Supervising, coaching, counselling, delegating, and motivating others. Developing and channelling the ideas and suggestions of the team.

Communication. The ability to convey and receive messages efficiently, both orally and in writing. Listening to the concerns of colleagues and customers. Handling customer complaints. Able to deal with difficult subordinates or customers. Presentation skills.

Influencing skills. Motivating and persuading colleagues. Changing people's mind sets. Promoting ideas, championing a cause and negotiating a solution.

Listing examples of your personal skills

The degree of personal skills required varies with job seniority level. However, most of these elements are required in every job. You need to determine the level for the vacancy. Think about situations from your previous experiences where you displayed each of these skills. For each of the personal skills above list two examples from your work experience. Memorise this list before the interview. Use these examples as evidence that you possess the required skills.

Think about the most likely interview questions. Insert these examples into your answers. Think about ways to add this information at the end of the interview. You may have to do this if the anticipated questions have not been asked. Refer to this list. Amend it if you later recall further supporting examples.

Demonstrate self awareness

Do not be discouraged if you lack some of the features of an ideal candidate. Everyone has their drawbacks. It is unlikely that the employer will find an ideal candidate. They are, after all, looking for the closest match. The critical thing is to recognise your shortcomings. Convince the interviewer that you will take steps to overcome them. Demonstrate a willingness to undertake training and additional study. Convince the interviewer that you regularly analyse your personal traits and work on self-improvement.

The reasoning behind the interviewer's questions

The interviewer will attempt to ascertain the following about each candidate:

- Skill level and competency.
- Range and scope of the candidate's work experience.
- How closely the candidate's competencies match the job requirements.
- Extent of previous achievements.
- Commitment to developing their career.
- Full understanding of the implications of doing the job.
- Ability to do the job.
- Ability to learn new tasks.
- Willingness to persevere and overcome difficulties.
- Ability to work well under pressure.
- Ability to meet deadlines.
- Ability to work unsupervised.
- Ability to set goals and willingness to follow through on them.
- Ability to solve problems.
- Willingness to show initiative.
- Tendency to set personal goals and review performance.
- Evidence of learning from mistakes.
- Reliability.
- Ability to add value to the organisation.
- Evidence that the job is the candidate's clear first choice.
- Level of enthusiasm.
- Level of motivation.
- Commitment to the role.
- Attention to detail.
- Suitability for the role.
- Compatibility with corporate ethos.
- Positive response to instructions and authority.
- Ability to build and maintain relationships with work colleagues.
- Ability to adapt to changing work conditions.
- Probability that they will remain with the company.

- Any discrepancy between answers.
- Signs that they are hiding anything.
- Signs of any negative traits that would exclude them.

The interviewer will review your past experience and job performance. He will take this as an indicator of future potential. He will try to envisage you in the job.

Desirable qualities

It is not just your responses that concern the interviewer. It is also how you present them. Can you analyse the issues, collect your thoughts and give a reasoned response? How do you interact while explaining, arguing or illustrating a point with examples? The interviewer wants to establish if you are mature, well balanced, reliable, responsible, trustworthy, enthusiastic, positive in outlook, logical, hard-working, loyal, co-operative and flexible.

These are all desirable characteristics. You should attempt to portray these characteristics through your answers. This will give you an advantage over the opposition. You will be more likely to receive the job offer.

Chapter 15. Types of interview

There are a number of different types of interview. In order to be short listed, you will have to employ a different strategy for each.

Screening interviews

A screening interview is a first stage interview. It is designed to create a short list of candidates for the next stage, which may be a second interview. A screening interview is designed to eliminate candidates lacking the minimum job requirements. Anyone displaying or revealing negative personal characteristics will be eliminated. If there is any doubt about a candidate's suitability he will be rejected.

Screening interviews are carried out by personnel managers or external recruitment agencies. The interviewers tend to be very experienced at what they do. The screener often has no detailed knowledge of the job requirements. Do not talk about technical issues if the immediate supervisor is not present. Save this for the second interview. Concentrate instead on demonstrating your matching personal skills, qualifications, achievements and potential.

The interviewer lacks the authority to hire candidates. His remit is simply to short list the best qualified candidates for the next stage. He is a gatekeeper. You will not pass unless he can verify your credentials. You must avoid all the common pitfalls that will cause you to be rejected.

Let the screener control the process. He is looking to tick a list of boxes to let you through to the next stage. Do not raise any new topics. This will only give the screener another avenue to go looking for negative information. You will make the cut if you can sell your matching skills.

Telephone screening

Up to a quarter of companies use telephone screening. Other companies employ agencies who use this practice. Some jobs, such as call centre operatives, involve using the phone a lot. Telephone screening is likely to be used as a first stage selection process for these jobs. The aim will be to reject anyone who lacks a good telephone manner.

The telephone screening interview should be arranged at a time that suits you. You may, however, receive an unexpected call from a company to which you have applied. If this happens, make an excuse and ask them to ring you back in say half an hour. Use the time to get your application folder. Read through it to refresh your memory.

A telephone interview might consist of questions to:

- Determine if you have the essential skills and qualifications.
- Confirm that you have other desired competencies.

You will not encounter an in-depth question and answer session. Employers prefer to do this in a face to face environment. This allows them to study body language as part of their decision making process.

When taking part in a telephone screening interview make sure that you:

- Use a land line, the signal is better and it is easier to concentrate.
- Turn off the call waiting facility so that you are not interrupted.
- Keep a glass of water at hand in case your mouth becomes dry.
- Have a pen and paper available to take notes.
- Keep your CV available to help you answer questions during the call.
- Keep a list of your matching skills to refer to when answering questions
- Answer the phone promptly.
- Speak slowly and clearly.
- Be courteous and polite.
- Use the interviewer's title and surname.

- Don't interrupt the interviewer.
- Sound enthusiastic.
- Smile, it makes you sound warmer and more relaxed.
- Do not any chew gum or food.
- Avoid interruptions from children, dogs, television, ringing mobile phones or door bells.

Milk round interviews

Milk round interviews are arranged by university careers offices. They invite local and national employers to their premises, usually twice a year. Employers send a personnel manager and a department manager to carry out on campus screening interviews. Successful candidates are invited to the next stage of the process. This might be a second interview, or attendance at an assessment centre.

Interviewers focus on academic achievements, core personal attributes, and evidence of drive and enthusiasm. They short list for the total annual graduate intake. There will be various vacancies in a number of different areas of the organisation. Your aim should be to secure a second interview. You should also find out which vacancies exist. This will help you prepare for the next stage.

Selection interviews - Second interviews

In a selection interview the interviewer has the power to hire you. You are a member of the pool of approved candidates, deemed capable of doing the job. Questions will be more job specific. The outcome of the selection interview will be a job offer for the successful candidate. For this type of interview you must go all out to sell your competency, your compatibility and your commitment to the role.

Second interviews are often held at the company premises. There are usually a number of interviewers present. This might include the personnel manager, the immediate supervisor and a senior manager wishing to assess candidates.

If you have been invited to a second interview the company already believes that you can do the job. You must reinforce this belief. You must do nothing to raise doubts about your suitability. The interviewer now wants to be reassured about two additional factors. Will you work hard? Will you fit in with colleagues and your new boss?

Before attending a second interview you must review your performance at the first interview. You should have carried out a post interview analysis on leaving the first interview. Advice on how to do this is given in Chapter 36. This will uncover areas where you did not perform well in the first interview. It will also reveal areas where the interviewer had concern about your suitability. At the second interview the interviewer will focus on these areas. This is where minor doubts still linger in regard to your suitability. If you can provide additional supporting evidence you will help alleviate these doubts.

Prepare extra supporting examples of your skill set for the second interview. One of the interviewer's may have been present at the first interview. It is not enough to repeat the answers you gave first time round. You need to up your performance with more examples.

Internal interviews

Find out as much as possible about internal vacancies in advance. Talk to the previous job holder if you can. If the job is new, talk to other people working in the department. You should not talk to the other applicants.

Prepare as you would for an external position. Match your competencies with the job requirements. List any transferable skills if applying to a different department.

Your current boss may be present at the interview. You may also know other panel members. However, you must behave as you would if applying for an external job elsewhere. Assume that the interviewers know nothing of your performance. Highlight all of your achievements and the benefits that accrued to the company.

Each panel member will mark you in isolation. Do not rely on your boss letting the other members know that you are a good employee. He will not want to show bias.

Competing with external candidates

As an internal candidate you may be competing with external applicants for a position.   You have a number of advantages over external applicants. First of all you already work for the company. You are aware of their operations. You know more about the job, the department, the new boss and the interviewers. Use this knowledge to your advantage during the interview. Subtly build and maintain rapport with the interviewers, particularly the immediate supervisor.

As an internal candidate you should use your insider knowledge as your main selling point. You can hit the ground running. You will produce results from day one. You do not need a period of induction. You do not require any training. You have all the necessary contacts within the company and with customers or suppliers. You know who to approach in the other departments to help projects along. You know how to get them on your side. You are aware of all the company procedures and policies. You already know the best way to get things done in this company. You have a proven track record. There is no risk associated with hiring you. You have already demonstrated your long term commitment to the company.

Point out any occasions when you covered for your boss or acted up temporarily. You were a safe pair of hands. You got the job done. You dealt with all the issues and coped with any pressure. You produced results. The company can rely on you to take things further if you are given the role permanently. You have several ideas you could introduce if you were given the authority to do so.

Limiting factors for internal candidates

The main disadvantage for an internal candidate is that you cannot overstate your current performance. Your company will be well aware of it.

Get a copy of your past appraisals from the personnel department. Note any criticism. All panel members will have read these appraisals as part of their preparation. They will focus on any weaknesses. If not they might be predisposed to marking you lower in these areas.

Focus on these shortcomings as part of your preparation. Show how you have overcome these weaknesses. Give practical examples of your achievements. Do this when asked about weak points or what you have learned from your mistakes. Never introduce any additional weak points that were not on your appraisals.

Unique issues affecting internal interviews

With internal promotion other factors are in play. The successful applicant must be replaced in his role. Your current boss may be concerned about replacing you, particularly if the vacancy is in a different department. He may have come to rely on you. Reassure your current boss in advance by saying that you would be happy to assist your replacement if appointed.

If applying to a different department, the manager in that area may favour one of his own subordinates. You must convince him of your suitability by stressing transferable skills. You must stress that your career aspirations lie in that area.

Finally the company may be tempted to appoint a compromise candidate. This may be someone in a position that will become redundant. This causes less overall disruption to the firm.

Stress interviews

Stress interviewing tactics may be used to see how candidates perform under pressure.

Tactics include:

- Dominating, aggressive interrogation.
- Deliberately awkward or embarrassing questions.
- Leading and negative questions.
- Taking up opposing views to the interviewee.
- Quick fire questions.
- Changing topic frequently.
- No logical sequence.
- Not allowing candidates to complete answers.
- Continual interruption.
- Challenging the candidate's answers or position.
- Ignoring the candidate's answers.
- Deliberately misinterpreting answers.
- Remaining silent when candidate has answered question.

Most people regard stress interviews as unprofessional. They do not give a favourable impression of the company. The interviewer's behaviour could fall foul of fair employment and anti-discrimination legislation.

Stress interviewing techniques do not help to select the right candidate. In fact the process is counter-productive. When faced with these tactics most candidates will be either hostile or defensive. They clam up. They do not establish rapport. They fail to communicate. Making an objective decision on who to employ under these conditions is extremely difficult.

No decent candidate wants to work for a company adapting these tactics. The employer should find out why the job contains such a stressful atmosphere. They should then rectify the situation, thus improving the working conditions for their existing employees.

If faced with these tactics remain calm, objective and polite. Ask for the relevance of the questioning technique. If you are not satisfied with the reply, state that you would like to terminate the interview. Get up and leave slowly. If you are not recalled immediately with an apology, follow up with a letter of complaint.

Do you want to work in such an environment for such a person? Would you rather not work for a company who treats you with a little more respect?

One-to-one interview

This type of interview usually makes it easier to build rapport with the interviewer. One-to-one interviews are normally screening interviews carried out by a personnel manager. The main problem is that they are open to claims of personal bias by the interviewer. The single interviewer needs to be skilled. There is no one else present to pick up on any issues from the candidate's response that he may miss.

Panel interviews

A panel interview consists of three or more interviewers. For certain job categories, such as teaching, the panel might have up to a dozen members. Panel interviews are favoured when the hiring decision affects several areas of the organisation. Certain service jobs, such as maintenance, interact with a number of different departments. For scientific, engineering or IT jobs a specialist panel member may be present. He will ask specialist-knowledge questions and score the answers to these questions.

Panel interviews are favoured by the civil service, local government, educational authorities and other public sector bodies. The results are viewed as less prone to individual bias, prejudice or subjectivity. The use of a panel also protects the company against claims of discrimination.

Educational authorities view your ability to present yourself to a panel as being representative of how you would deal with a classroom full of students. Presentation skills will be a determining factor in their judgements.

The panel usually contains a chairman. The chairman will introduce the other panel members. He is responsible for ensuring that the interview stays on track and on schedule. The chairman also ensures that each candidate is treated fairly.

Individual panel members ask questions on one aspect of the candidate's background. They also ask questions about how the role will interact with their area of responsibility. They will, however, score candidates on their total performance.

Many people find panel interviews intimidating. There seems to be a barrage of questions coming from all directions. There is often no logical flow in the sequencing of the questions. Larger panels can feel more like a tribunal sitting in judgement. It takes longer to get settled. Questions can be more demanding. Each panel member will be asking questions about his own area of expertise.

It is difficult to build any form of rapport as you are only asked one or two questions by each interviewer in turn. There can be interplay between panel members who may be more interested in individual point scoring.

Dealing with panel interviews

You must appreciate that all candidates face the same circumstances. In addition the panel interview is more objective.

At the beginning establish the roles of the panel members. Find out who is the supervisor for the vacant position. Concentrate on building rapport with this person. He will have the most influence on the final selection. Too many candidates concentrate on the chairman. This is a critical error. The chairman has little input in the decision making process. He may not even score candidates.

Reply to the person asking the question in each case. Then use gestures and eye contact to include the other panel members. Imagine that you are talking to an audience. Speak a little louder than normal. Ask your own questions as the interview progresses.

Do not say anything that favours one department while presenting concerns for another. Talk about things that will benefit the company as a whole. Panel members are drawn from several departments. Each has their own departmental interests and priorities.

Some panel members will seem more reticent and less receptive than others. This can be quite disconcerting. However it usually has nothing to do with your performance. It is just a reflection of the different personalities involved. It might be a consequent of inter-departmental rivalry. Ignore these distractions. Concentrate on the task at hand.

Direct your final questions to the chairman unless it is obvious which panel member should answer an individual question.

Multiple mini interviews (MMI) – Medical school application

Multiple mini interviews are used for graduates seeking entry into medical or dentistry courses at UK universities. Before being invited to the MMI you must have sat and passed an admission test for UK medical schools such as the UKCAT test. All UK students make their university application through the Universities & Colleges Admissions Service (UCAS).

Candidates will be invited to medical school interview on the basis of their:

- UKCAT or other admission test score.
- Personal statement.
- Academic achievement to date and predicted final results.
- School reference.
- UCAS application form score – marked on certain relevant criteria.

The UCCAS and personal statements must demonstrate that the candidate possesses certain desirable qualities. These include communication skills, empathy and teamwork. There should also be evidence of commitment to medicine through work placement. The applicant must demonstrate an appreciation of the requirements of training for and practising medicine.

MMI candidates take part in a series of short or mini interviews one after another in a timed circuit. Each interview lasts less than ten minutes. There are usually between 6 and 8 interviews to complete. At each interview station the candidate faces a different task. Assessors are present at each station. They score candidates on their performance. Before participating at each station the candidates may be given instructions relating to the task and two minutes to prepare.

A couple of stations will consist of one-to-one interviews. One station might cover reasons for wanting to study medicine and become a doctor. A second might cover the candidate's personal statement. A third might ask competency based questions to determine if the candidate has the right personal qualities.

At least one station will present a typical moral dilemma confronting doctors. Candidates are asked how they would deal with such a situation. There may be a station which involves the candidate's ability to reason and communicate. This could involve instructing an actor on how to carry out a cumbersome task.

One station might present a role playing exercise. You will be dealing with an actor playing the part of a patient or a relative. You may have to break some bad news, or show empathy for someone in distress.

Some universities also use group exercises. This enables them to assess your team working and communication skills. Advice on dealing with group exercises is included in the next section.

Assessment of MMI performance is based on the following criteria:

- Commitment to medicine as a career.
- Medical work experiences in first aid, hospitals, care homes, etc.
- Understanding of the core qualities and role of a doctor.
- Background reading and understanding of medical issues.

- Knowledge of medical history, the NHS and current medical news stories.
- Knowledge of the university course.
- Ability to deal with stress.
- Empathy or evidence of concern for the welfare of others.
- Honesty and trustworthiness.
- Moral reasoning.
- Critical thinking which is essential in diagnosing patient's condition.
- Problem solving, another essential for diagnosis.
- Ability to multi-task.
- Ability to move directly from one problem to another
- Communication skills, particularly listening, which is essential on picking up cues from patients that might help diagnose the root problem.
- Interpersonal skills - ability to relate to a wide and diverse group of people.
- Professionalism or maturity.
- Team working skills – essential in medicine practice, where you need to work with many health care professionals specialising in different areas affecting your patient's care.

Assessment centres

The use of assessment centres is expensive. For this reason they tend to be used as a second stage selection procedure. They are used by companies to fill several vacancies at the same time. Assessment centres are regularly used by larger firms for their annual graduate intake. Short listed candidates from the milk round are invited to attend. Public sector organisations such as the police force also favour their use.

A number of the short listed candidates are asked to attend the same session. Candidates could spend as much as two or three days at an assessment centre. The assessment centre might be hosted at the employer's site, a conference centre or a hotel.

Candidates undertake a series of individual and group exercises, tests and interviews. The aim is to emulate work related tasks. The goal is to assess the candidate's performance against certain key job related competencies. Several assessors will be used for each test. This reduces personal bias. Assessors can observe a number of candidates at the same time.

Companies use assessment centres because:

- The results tend to be fair and objective.
- There is a longer time frame to assess candidates.
- The results tend to be a more accurate predictor of future performance.
- They accurately predict behaviour in a team or group environment.
- It gives candidates more information about the firm. This helps them decide whether or not the job is right for them. This should reduce turnover.

The following exercises are often used:

- Psychometric tests.
- In-tray exercises.
- Case studies.
- Group discussions.
- Group problem solving exercises.
- Team projects.
- Role-playing.
- Presentations.
- Interviews.
- Personality questionnaires.

In-tray exercises

With an in-tray exercise you will be presented with a list of tasks. You must prioritise them in a given time frame. You may have to draft brief replies to memos, decide on tasks to delegate, or recommend action to your boss. The aim of the test is to simulate actual work tasks. These tests are designed to evaluate if you can:

- Follow written instructions.

- Assimilate information.
- Work on your own.
- Distinguish between important and irrelevant information.
- Make judgement calls.
- Prioritise tasks.
- Plan and organise your work.
- Manage your time.
- Pay attention to detail.
- Communicate your results in writing.

You may be required to type e-mails or answer calls as part of the exercise.

If carrying out this type of test you need to:

- Read all instructions carefully before you begin the tasks.
- Skim through all the documents and sort into broad categories.
- Identify the critical or urgent items.
- Tackle the urgent items first.
- Prioritise the remaining items.
- Follow any guideline notes left by your fictional boss.
- Monitor your remaining time as you work through the exercise.

Case Studies

You may be given a case study to complete. It may be an individual or a group task. You will be presented with a folder of information from a fictional company or department. You will be given a set time to complete a number of questions. The information will be much more detailed than you need. It will contain some trivial or irrelevant information. The information may be presented in written, tabular and graphic format.

You will be assessed on your ability to:

- Absorb a lot of information in a short time span.
- Extract what is relevant in the short time available.
- Analyse and interpret data.
- Organise the relevant information.

- Plan and present information in the requested format.
- Produce results of an acceptable standard.
- Complete the task in the time available.

 If you are running out of time near the end make a note of how you would have completed the task, if time permitted. This might get you some additional marks that you otherwise would miss.

If the case study is given to a group be aware that you might not all have been presented with the same information. Each member of the group may have been given some unique insight into the problem. Establish if this is the case at the outset. Delegate different tasks to each member, in order to complete the exercise on time. Allow time before the end for the results to be discussed by the whole group. Incorporate any amendments before compiling the answers. In a group setting the assessors will also be judging role playing, time management and interaction between the participants.

Role Play

In this type of test you will be asked to pretend you are in a given role. You will have to deal with a certain person, in a given situation. For example you may be a customer service employee dealing with an irate customer. The customer will be played by one of the assessors. Alternatively you may be asked to be a salesman dealing with a client.

The situation will simulate typical job related tasks. You will be assessed on how you interact. You will also be scored on your ability to cope with unexpected developments.

If you are invited to an assessment centre think about the nature of the role play you are likely to encounter. Prepare in advance for the type of inter play you anticipate. Rehearse your arguments and your responses to the likely tactics the assessor will take.

Advice on participating in group exercises

In group exercises you are not in direct competition with the other participants. Many of them will be applying to other areas of the firm. You may be taking part in several exercises with these group members over a few days. You must build friendships and a good working relationship. You will be under scrutiny the whole time. Your team working skills will be a major part of the selection decision.

Groups are meant to work collectively towards a common goal. Effective teams consist of participants with a variety of skills. Group members have various roles to play. Some of these are:

- Leader, co-ordinator, initiator, implementer, finisher, research person, ideas person, facilitator, chairman, secretary, analyst, team worker or specialist.

You may be assigned a specific role before the test begins. In this case you must demonstrate the appropriate traits. More often the group is left leaderless. The assessors want to see who emerges as the natural leader. They will look to see what roles the other participants adopt.

Participants are often judged solely on their behaviour. The outcome of the exercise is irrelevant. The company is more concerned on how you interact with others. They will judge your body language, communication skills and empathy with other team members. They will look at factors such as decisiveness, initiative, assertiveness, leadership, analytical ability, diplomacy, cooperation, reasoning and maturity. They will also take into account what you contribute in terms of ideas and rational suggestions. Did you assist the group to meet its targets? Were you a help or a hindrance to progress?

Tactics to employ in group exercises

Adapt the following tactics when participating in group exercises:

- Do not attempt to dominate the proceedings.
- Get involved and contribute ideas.

- Do not verbally attack other members of the group.
- Do not get involved in arguments.
- Keep any criticism constructive.
- Be assertive if required.
- Try to resolve conflicts between other members of the group.
- Do not prevent others from speaking.
- Do not interrupt others.
- Always use a rational line of argument.
- Keep to the facts where possible.
- Present both sides of the argument before opting for a solution.
- If appointed leader, encourage participation from everyone before making decisions.
- If appointed chairman, keep the group focused and on target against time constraints.
- Summarize the issues to date.
- Be aware of the time limits.
- Remind the group of their goal.
- Be sure to complete the task in the allotted time.

Presentations

You may be asked to give a presentation of your choice. More likely you will be asked to prepare one on a set topic. You may be given a fixed time to analyse certain information. You then have to give a presentation to a group of assessors. You will usually be asked to use simple aids, such as a flip chart and markers.

You may be asked for instance to recommend an investment for new facilities. You may be given a number of alternatives. Present your case along the following lines:

- Introduce yourself. Thank the audience for attending.
- Set the scene with an opening statement.
- Clearly define the topic. Include a short heading.
- Give a brief introduction outlining the problem and the objectives.
- Outline what you are going to cover.
- Define the scope of the problem and who will be affected.
- State the issues as you see them.

- Show the alternatives that you have considered.
- Outline the pros and cons of each.
- State your findings.
- Give a logical reasoning for your decision.
- Outline any risk involved.
- Outline the costs to the organisation.
- Quantify the benefits.
- Give a time line for introduction.
- Specify the likely payback period.
- Summarise your main conclusions.
- Wrap up with a closing statement.
- Invite and answer questions.

Regardless of the presentation topic you need to follow these guidelines:

- Keep it simple and to the point.
- Do not try to cover too much material.
- Do not over run your time slot.
- Stand up when giving your presentation.
- Do not walk in front of the chart or screen.
- Move about a little. Avoid standing behind desks or lecterns.
- Speak clearly, speak up and vary the pitch of your voice.
- Make it interesting.
- Smile and inject enthusiasm into your presentation.
- Include the whole audience. Vary your eye contact.
- Have a clear beginning, middle and end.
- Present the key points in a logical sequence.
- Use bullet points to present information simply and clearly.
- Do not rely too much on notes.
- Do not read from the screen or the board. Paraphrase and expand on the displayed material. - Design the bullet points to prompt your memory.
- Pitch it at the comprehension level of your audience.
- Focus the content on the concerns of the audience.
- Address individuals by name.
- Let the audience know when they can ask questions.
- Anticipate the likely questions. Rehearse your answers.
- Repeat your conclusions at the end to reinforce your main points.

- Finish on an upbeat point.

You may know in advance that you will be expected to give a presentation. If you know the topic, then prepare and rehearse it in advance. The more you can rehearse the better.

Chapter 16. Interviewing techniques

Interviewers pose their questions in a number of different ways. They have specific reasons for doing this.

Open ended questions

Open ended questions are designed to encourage candidates to talk. They cannot be answered with a simple 'yes' or 'no'. They are used to elicit information about the candidate. Open ended questions are not restrictive. They give the candidate a degree of latitude in his response. An example of an open ended question would be 'What are your strong points?' In most situations interviewers prefer to use open ended questions.

Closed questions

A closed question is one that can only be answered with a simple 'yes' or 'no'.
You should not be asked many closed questions at an interview. There are a few exceptions to this. The interviewer may ask a closed question when seeking clarification of personal details. He may also ask a closed question to verify his interpretation of something. For example he may ask you to confirm if he should use your mobile phone number to contact you.

An inexperienced interviewer may ask you a closed question by mistake. In this case you need to expand your answer. Just treat the question as if it was an open ended one.

Wide open questions

Wide open questions have little definition or constraint. You are given a free hand to express yourself in any way you like. This type of question can be answered in a multitude of ways, on a wide range of topics. An example would be 'Tell me a little about yourself.'

Questions are deliberately posed in this way to see if you will stray off on a tangent. Stick to the point when answering this type of question. Remember you are at a meeting. The purpose is to discuss your suitability for the role. Every answer should be aimed at matching your competencies to the job requirements. Ask for clarification if you need it before you answer.

Probing questions

Interviewers use probing questions to elicit additional information on a given topic. There could be two opposing reasons for using probing questions.

First of all, the interviewer may be trying to give you a fair chance. He is prompting you for additional supporting information. You have not answered the initial question well enough. However the interviewer believes, from your application, that you must possess additional competencies in this area. He is encouraging you to sell yourself better. You can usually detect this by observing the interviewer's body language. He might smile, nod his head or show empathy. You must expand with more supporting information. The onus is on you. The interviewer will only help you so much.

Alternatively the interviewer may be trying to unearth weaknesses that will cause you to be rejected. You may have said something to arise his suspicion. You may have contradicted an earlier answer. Perhaps you are exaggerating some competency? Again look out for the tell-tale body language. Is he frowning? Has he raised an eyebrow? Does he look surprised or quizzical? You are entering dangerous territory. Be careful how you proceed.

Probing questions can also be used to interrupt and get you back on track. You may have drifted into areas that are not relevant to the interviewer.

Leading questions

Leading questions are used by interviewers to lead you in a particular direction. Usually you need to go in the opposite direction! An example might be 'You didn't achieve much in your last job. Did you?' It could be that the interviewer has formed an opinion that you need to change. For example he might say 'You seem to be a bit overqualified. Don't you?' This indicates that you are in danger of being rejected. You must now provide examples from your experience to make the interviewer revise his opinion of you.

In some cases the leading question is asked of all candidates. It is employed as a deliberate tactic to undermine candidates and force them into revealing weaknesses. It might be used to imply that you are lacking basic skills. Perhaps you are exaggerating a given competency.

Stand your ground. Do not admit to anything that is being suggested. If the interviewer has definite information, then let him produce it. He is trying to throw you off guard. In the process he hopes to get you to admit to weaknesses. This will help him to eliminate you from the process.

Just ask him to be specific. If he cannot articulate his problem, then you have no case to answer. If he has a specific concern, then you can address it directly.

The calculated pause

Sometimes the interviewer will deliberately remain silent after you have finished answering a question. The implication being that you have not answered well enough. This is unnerving and many applicants fall into the trap of continuing to speak. They become flustered and embarrassed. They rush in to fill the void. This causes them to stray from the topic. They might repeat what they have already said. Worst of all they may reveal something negative about themselves.

You may encounter this tactic after being asked a negative or leading question. Remain silent and wait the interviewer out. He is controlling the interview. If he wants more information, let him ask for it. If the silence becomes unbearable, then just ask him if he has another question he would like to ask. This reinforces the fact that you believe you have already answered the last question well enough.

Hypothetical questions

Hypothetical or 'what if' questions are based on imaginary situations or problems that you might encounter in the role. Hypothetical questions help the interviewer to determine your values. They are used to assess your thought processes in terms of problem solving, analytical and reasoning skills. You will be asked how you would react under a given set of circumstances. Hypothetical questions have one major drawback. Candidates will describe the required behavioural traits. There is no guarantee that they will actually behave in this manner in real life circumstances.

You may be asked a work related hypothetical question. Consider the reason for the question. What is the issue? What behaviour would be expected from you under these circumstances? If you can, answer using an actual example from your experience. Supply supporting information. Show that you were logical in your approach. You worked through the problem. You considered your options and came to an informed decision.

If given a hypothetical problem with insufficient background information, ask for further clarification. The interviewer may be testing to see if you would jump to conclusions without having sufficient evidence. You may be told that there is no further information available. In this case just say that you would normally obtain more information before taking action. Explain the action you would take and the set of circumstances that would cause you to take this action. Specify how your actions might differ under different circumstances.

Biographical based approach

This type of interviewing style was favoured in the past. The interviewer used the candidate's application or CV as a template. He would then go through their career from start to finish. The idea was to flesh out the bones of the CV. Questions tended to focus on likes and dislikes and reasons for changing career direction. The candidate was judged on the relevance of his experience to the advertised role. The interviewer asked additional questions on interpersonal skills to help determine suitability.

The behavioural approach – competency based interviewing

Competency based interviews are sometimes referred to as behavioural interviews. In this type of interview you are asked about actual situations you have dealt with in the past. Past behaviour is believed to be a better indicator of future job performance.

Competencies are particular skills required to carry out job related tasks to an acceptable standard. The company will draw up a competency framework for each different job. This will include those skills which are essential to be successful in the role. Competencies can be either behavioural or task related.

Employers focus on the following behavioural competencies:

- Work ethic.
- Communication skills.
- Initiative.
- Planning and organising.
- Problem solving.
- Analysing data.
- Strategic thinking.
- Interpersonal skills.
- Team work.
- Leadership.
- Negotiating.
- Overcoming adversity.
- Dealing with stress.
- Working with difficult colleagues or customers.
- Customer service.
- Fostering relationships.
- Motivating and developing others.

The technique enables the interviewer to probe deeper into actual circumstances. He will be able to assess how the candidate dealt with actual problems. It is easier to determine if the candidate is telling the truth. The interviewer can judge the extent of the candidate's knowledge, skills, reasoning and behaviour. He can assess whether the candidate's skill set is appropriate for the role.

Approach to answering competency based questions

Do not talk in broad, generalised terms about how you might deal with a problem. Give a specific example from your experience. Talk in the first person about your individual contributions. Be prepared. Anticipate the probing questions.

When answering competency based questions give details on:

- The problem you encountered.
- The options you considered.
- The rationale behind your decision making.
- How you implemented the solution.
- How you consulted your boss on major issues.
- The lessons you learned from the problem.
- How you might tackle the problem differently with the benefit of hindsight.
- How you can implement similar solutions in the advertised role.

Chapter 17. The day of the interview

Supporting information to bring to the interview

For certain jobs you may be requested to bring supporting evidence with you to interview. Examples include artwork, photographs or technical drawings. In any case you should always bring a file with the following:

- Original copies of examination or qualification certificates.
- Written references or testimonials.
- Additional copies of your CV.
- Your covering letter.
- Portfolios of your work.
- Any work permits if required.
- A good quality pen.
- A writing pad to take notes.

Getting to the interview on time

Never, ever arrive late for your interview. Being late shows a lack of respect for the employer. It also suggests a lack of motivation. If you show up late for the interview, it will be assumed that you will do likewise for the job itself.

Plan your route in advance. Aim to get there about thirty minutes early. Check out in advance which entrance you are expected to use. Find out where the nearest available parking is located. You may have to sign in at the gate, and then park your vehicle, before checking in at reception. This process could take ten minutes or longer. You should arrive at reception fifteen minutes before the scheduled time.

Leave early if you are driving. This will compensate for possible traffic jams, or parking issues. If the job is close by, then travel to it some days earlier at the scheduled time. This will let you know how long the journey will take by your chosen route, under the same conditions.

If you are travelling by public transport then take an early train or bus. This will compensate for any delays in service.

Taking these precautions will help avoid anxiety. This enables you to arrive early and in the correct frame of mind. You can then concentrate on the interview itself. Arriving late and flustered gives the wrong first impression.

You may, despite all your precautions, still be running late. Make sure you have brought along the company phone number. Ring up, apologise and reschedule if possible. Blame an unforeseen event, such as a road closure.

If you cannot attend on the scheduled date, ring up and reschedule. Do this immediately upon receiving the invite. Make sure your reason for doing this is not trivial.

Arriving at the premises

Never bring anyone with you to the interview. If someone is with you, let them wait outside the premises. When you arrive at security, or reception, introduce yourself. Give the details of your interview, including the interviewer's name.

Waiting at reception

You will usually need to wait at reception until you are called for interview. Be polite and pleasant to any members of staff you encounter. Any impoliteness could be reported later to the interviewer.

Leave overcoats, bags or umbrellas at reception. Only take your folder with your supporting documents into the interview room. Switch off your mobile phone when you arrive at reception. Do not turn it on again until you have left the building.

If you arrive early, freshen and tidy up and check your appearance. Take a sip of water if your mouth is dry. You can then review your interview preparation notes or check your CV. Some people prefer to relax and free their mind of all anxiety.

Additional company information at reception

You can use the remaining time to read any brochures in the reception area. These often contain information about the company and the industry. There may also be awards or certificates displayed in this area. You could refer to them when answering questions about the company.

Ignore the competition

Do not get into a conversation with other candidates. Instead review your notes or relax and get into the correct frame of mind. Do not worry about the quality of the other candidates. Concentrate instead on preparing your case.

Making an entrance

Knock and wait for an answer before entering the interview room. Close the door behind you. Walk in confidently. One of the interviewers will take the lead role by introducing himself and everyone else. Smile, say hello and shake hands. Thank him for inviting you to the interview.

Introductions

Shake hands and smile at everyone he introduces. Look people in the eyes when you shake hands. Do not look down. This will appear submissive.

You should have got the names of the interviewers in advance as part of your research. However last minute replacements can be seconded onto interview panels. Repeat each person's name as they are introduced. This helps you to remember their names. You should refer to everyone by their correct name and title throughout the interview.

It should be obvious which your seat is. Walk over to it. Wait to be invited before sitting down. If you are not told to sit, then politely ask if you should sit there. If there is a choice of seats chose the one nearest to the interviewers.

Try to appear comfortable and relaxed and pleased to be there.

The structure of the interview

The interviewer will start by welcoming you and introducing the panel. He will attempt to put you at ease by commenting on the weather. He may ask about your journey to the interview. Keep your answer short and polite. Remember to smile. Do not get into a prolonged conversation. Your aim is to secure the job. Do not waste valuable interview time.

The interviewer will explain the interview structure. He will indicate how long it should take. He will adhere closely to his prepared interview schedule. He will go through your application form or CV. He will ask questions on your education, qualifications, training and work experiences. He will seek clarification on certain aspects of your application. He will ask questions about any career gaps. He may ask about interests outside of work and your present circumstances. He will ask about your knowledge of the company and the job. At each stage he will gauge your competencies by matching them to the specified requirements.

The interviewer will explain more about the company. He will explain the terms and conditions. He may ask for evidence of your work or qualifications. He might ask for details of referees. He will give you the opportunity to ask questions. By the end of the interview both parties should know enough to make an informed decision. The company will have decided whether or not you are suitable for the position. Similarly you should know if the job is suitable.

On closing the interview, the interviewer will let you know when you should hear from the company.

The harmful effect of interview nerves

Many people dread the thought of attending an interview. Interview nerves can hinder the performance of even the best candidates. A great deal rests on a successful outcome. Future job security, earnings and prospects are all in the balance. It is something we need to get right.

Nerves can help the adrenaline to flow and benefit our performance. However uncontrolled anxiety can have the opposite effect. The desire to create a good impression unsettles some candidates. Fear is the root cause of this anxiety. Fear of the unknown and fear of messing up hampers their performance.

Most people worry about the questions the interviewer will ask. They don't wish to appear foolish by stumbling on an answer. Perfectly capable candidates can suddenly get flustered. They become self-conscious and embarrassed. They stumble on their words. They might even say things they do not mean. Worst of all they become tongue tied. All of this makes them appear unsuitable and leads to rejection.

Overcoming interview nerves

All of these concerns are natural emotions. However interviews are not meant to be an ordeal. They are basically a match making process where information and values are exchanged. The interviewer is simply searching for a candidate who can bring value to the company and who will be happy in the job.

The solution to avoiding excessive interview nerves is to carry out thorough preparation in advance. This helps you to anticipate the questions. You can then prepare the best possible answers based on your circumstances. Prepare a competency list of your accomplishments. Practise rehearsing your answers in advance.

Proper preparation enhances your self-confidence. It enables you to make a favourable impression. Positive thoughts produce positive results. Any initial nerves will disappear as you get under way with your answers. Interviewers will be impressed with your preparation and your confidence.

Appreciate your position

You must appreciate that you are beginning from a position of strength. The employer already believes that you have the essential skills to do the job. Otherwise you would not have been invited to the interview. If you lack the minimum requirements your application would have been rejected. Instead, you are now one of a select few. The number of competitors for the position has reduced dramatically. You are on the inside track. You are a potential new recruit.

The employer knows more about the job than you do. If they believe in your ability then why should you have any self-doubt? Now is your time to shine. You have made your entrance. Now you must give the performance that they have been waiting on.

Chapter 18. Interview protocol

At the interview you must behave in a professional manner. You need to be pleasant, agreeable and responsive. You must also be friendly, positive and confident. You need to project energy and enthusiasm. You must promote all your positive aspects. You must play down any negative traits. You must sell yourself and your potential.

It is important to observe the correct interview protocol. How you say things is just as important as what you say. Your body language needs to reinforce what you are saying. If not, the interviewer will pick up on this. He will develop a nagging doubt about your performance. He will have a gut feeling that something is not right. You will not get the job offer.

Appearance and first impressions

First impressions are critical. Interviewers will be influenced by the first impression you give, which is your appearance. They will have formed an opinion on you before you open your mouth. Personal grooming, hygiene and proper dress code are critical. First impressions are often inaccurate. However they are difficult to change. You never get a second chance to make a first impression. This is why your appearance needs to be professional.

Ensuring a good appearance

You will be judged on your appearance. If your appearance is poor, the interviewer will assume that your performance will also be substandard. A good appearance is critical in certain jobs. This includes anyone representing the company by dealing with clients, customers, suppliers or the public.

Advice on dress code for men

- Hair, finger nails, shoes and clothes should all be neat, clean and tidy.

- Hair should be recently cut for the interview.
- Wear a traditional two piece business suit and quality tie.
- Shirts should be pressed.
- Shoes should be new and polished.
- Face should be clean shaven, or beard or moustache neatly trimmed.
- Wear a long sleeve shirt.
- Do not wear any visible body piercings or ear rings.
- Keep your jacket on during the interview.

Advice on dress code for women

- Hair, finger nails, shoes and clothes should all be neat, clean and tidy.
- Wear a dress, skirt or suit.
- Skirts should cover your knees when standing and your thighs when seated.
- Do not wear a lot of jewellery.
- Do not wear large distracting jewellery.
- Keep make-up to a sensible level.
- Do not wear any visible body piercings apart from ear studs.

Clothing

Your appearance needs to be professional looking. Purchase the best quality clothing and shoes that you can afford. Make sure your clothing fits you well. Wear conservative dark colours such as black or navy. Never wear anything more casual than you would be expected to wear on the job. Do not wear winter clothing in summer, or vice versa. If you are attending a second interview, wear something different from the first occasion.

Do not wear something that is too warm, too tight or too revealing. Select natural fabrics like cotton, wool or silk. Arrange and try on your outfit the night before the interview. This will let you know if there are any issues. You do not want a panic on the morning of the interview.

Bring an overcoat and umbrella in case it rains. You will need to walk from security or the car park to the reception area. You do not want to turn up soaking wet. Make sure you bring a handkerchief to the interview.

Make sure you do not smell of alcohol or tobacco. Do not chew gum or anything else.

Body Language

Body language is a form of non verbal communication. Your body language reveals a lot about you. Experienced interviewers can interpret body language signals. They study your appearance and manner, posture, facial expression and eye contact. The signals they pick up may conflict with what you are saying. They can tell when something just doesn't look right. These non verbal cues will influence the interviewer's final decision

Below are just some examples of what the interviewer can detect from various body language cues:

Facial expressions - neutral, amused, disapproving, angry, surprised, embarrassed, concerned, sad, shocked, shy, paying attention, ready to speak.
Eye movement - receptive, evasive, lying, remembering, imagining, disapproving, aggressive, uncertain.
Posture - bored, tired, relaxed, anxious, apprehensive, confident, superior, interested, frustrated.
Gestures - thinking, disbelief, frustrated, remorse, apprehensive, sincere, open, innocent, low self-esteem, considering options, indecisive.
Voice - Anger, remorse, uncertainty, fear, forgetful, enthusiastic, bored, tired.
Movement - dominance, assertiveness, avoidance, anticipation, submission, doubt, lying, impatience, confidence.
Touch - reassurance, sincerity, warning, challenge, commiseration, praise.
Appearance – status, degree of care, self-esteem.

Body language is critical at interviews. Some researchers say that the spoken words only account for 7% of the message we are conveying. Visual cues account for 55% of the message. The remaining 38% is interpreted from the manner in which we say things.

Your body language is just as important as what you actually say. Your body language needs to reinforce the messages you are attempting to send. This takes practice. Carry out and record mock interviews. Review them paying close attention to your body language.

Adapt the correct posture

Sit upright during the interview. Do not slouch or sprawl. If your chair is facing the interviewer turn it slightly to the side. When answering questions lean forward slightly. This will make you look interested and attentive. Avoid leaning backwards as this suggests that you are disinterested. Moving your chair back suddenly suggests that you are uncomfortable with the question. Do not shift about in your chair. This gives the impression of nervousness, irritation or boredom.

Minimise gestures

Use your hands to illustrate your key points, but avoid over gesticulating. Keep them relaxed on your lap when the interviewer is speaking. Don't cross them defensively in front of you. Do not grip the arms of the chair tightly. This will make you appear tense and worried.

Remain relaxed but attentive. Do not fidget. Do not tap your feet. Do not drum your fingers on the desk. These are signs of boredom. Do not fiddle with your hair or jewellery. Do not bite your nails, or scratch your head. This will distract the interviewer.

Do not speak with your hands in front of your mouth. Do not touch your face. Touching the nose or mouth can be interpreted as a sign of someone who is lying.

Show that you are actively listening by nodding at appropriate intervals.

Maintain eye contact

Establish and maintain eye contact with the interviewer. Good eye contact gives the appearance of confidence and honesty. You should look at the interviewer most of the time when you are talking. However it is normal to look away when thinking about what you should say next.

Do not suddenly look away when asked a question. This suggests you are evading the issue. Avoiding eye contact completely when you are speaking is a sign of not telling the whole truth.

Do not stare incessantly at the interviewer. This looks confrontational and unnatural. It can be unnerving and distracting.

Vary your speech

You should speak clearly, audibly and distinctly. You should sound confident and enthusiastic when talking about the job, your strengths and your interests.

Introduce inflection into your speech and vary the pitch to show interest. Emphasise key words. Use short pauses between sentences.

Avoid mumbling and hesitation. These are signs that you are being evasive or untruthful. A monotone voice implies boredom or lack of interest.

Control facial expressions

Interviewers can tell a lot from facial expressions. We learn facial expressions as a baby, before we learn to talk. Facial expressions often reveal what we are trying to conceal. Facial expressions mirror our thoughts, feelings and emotions. This is caused by involuntary muscle reaction.

Remember to smile when you are introduced. This projects enthusiasm and sincerity and will give a good first impression.

Beware of sending the wrong signals with your facial expressions. A fixed lifeless expression suggests boredom. If you profess to be interested in a given topic, then make sure you look and sound enthusiastic.

A frown or grimace when asked a question suggests that you have something to hide. If you are relaxed, interested and attentive this will show in your face.

Mirror the interviewer's body language

Mirroring the interviewer's body language can help you build rapport. You should also smile when he does. Just make sure that any attempt to mirror body language does not interfere with active listening to what the interviewer is saying.

Be careful not to mirror the body language of the interviewer if it is not appropriate. If he slouches or sprawls, or puts his hands behind the back of his head, do not copy him.

Be honest

If you are being evasive, the interviewer may detect this in your expression. He will dig deeper, but if you are still reticent, he will drop the issue. He will come to the most obvious conclusion, that you are not telling the truth.

It is therefore better to be honest about a minor weakness, if you feel the interviewer is obviously suspicious. Explain how you are working to improve it. This is better than the interviewer thinking that you are hiding some major fault. Lies are regularly detected due to conflicting evidence or evasive behaviour. If a suspicion remains that you are not being truthful you will be rejected.

Chapter 19. Advice on answering interview questions

Interview structure

The interview will follow a structured, systematic pattern. Each candidate will be asked questions from an identical list. The list will cover education, qualifications, training, work experience, personal traits and possibly interests and hobbies. The interviewer will reserve some time to follow up on your answers. He will probe deeper where he feels it is appropriate. If there appear to be discrepancies in your answers the interviewer will investigate further.

Prepare your own answers to common interview questions

The interview is the worst place to work out the ideal answer to a question. The vast majority of interview questions can be anticipated. There should be only one or two interview questions that you have not anticipated.

The following chapters contain the most common interview questions. In each case the reasoning behind the questions has been provided. Guidelines are provided on the most appropriate answer. You are also advised on what not to say.

There are no set correct answers. Your answers need to be right for your own particular circumstances, skills and experiences. They need to be tailored to the job requirements. If you follow the advice provided you will be able to construct the correct answers for your circumstances. With each answer include a practical example to substantiate your claims.

Copy out each of these questions in turn. Consider your experiences and construct your own answers to each question. Use as many examples from your more recent work experience as possible. This process will take some time. However it is essential if you really want to secure the job offer. Construct your answers to match the job requirements. A lot of the groundwork you do can be used for future interviews.

Keep your answers concise, coherent, relevant and enthusiastic. Plan to spend no more than two minutes on each answer. You can elaborate if prompted by the interviewer.

Anticipate the questions

Given the wide variety of jobs and interview formats it is not possible to list all the likely questions. Every interview is different. The questions you will be asked will vary slightly. In order to anticipate the likely questions you need to put yourself in the interviewer's shoes.

Study your CV or application. Think about the job requirements. Where do you match the requirements closely and where do you appear to have any weaknesses? If the interviewer suspects that you are weak in a particular area, he will probe for more information. Consider where your CV is not a strong match in terms of job requirements. Now concentrate on strengthening your case in these areas.

Are there any obvious gaps in your CV? Expect the interviewer to probe deeper in these areas. With the proper preparation, you will be able to tackle most questions.

Be prepared to talk about your career choices

Interviewers tend to ask about choices you made that caused your education or career to change direction. They are interested in what motivates you. They want to be reassured that you had a clear, logical, consistent, long term career plan. Think about the likely questions they will ask, given your CV or application. Prepare appropriate answers.

What you must *do* when answering interview questions:

- Remain calm and composed.
- Concentrate on what you are being asked.
- Establish and maintain eye contact with the interviewers.
- Take your time. Listen carefully and consider the issues before answering each question.
- Do not answer a question until you understand the reason behind it. If you are not sure, ask   for clarification. It is better to do this than give a poor, irrelevant or partial answer.
- Answer the question you were asked. Listen carefully to how the question is posed.
- Vary your speech pattern. Talk clearly and distinctly.
- Be positive, businesslike, professional, confident, pleasant and enthusiastic throughout.
- Smile. Be friendly and polite. Use the interviewer's name.
- Use positive language with action verbs.
- Keep your answers short and relevant. Aim for less than two minutes.
- Talk in the first person. Stress your personal contributions to the team
- Compliment the firm occasionally.
- Introduce supporting information with every answer.
- Give brief, practical examples from your work experience.
- Quantify your achievements in terms of benefits to your employer.
- Sell your skills, experience, accomplishments and potential.
- Relate every answer to the job requirements. Explain the benefits you can bring to the role.
- Tell the truth, but emphasise your positive attributes.
- Ask relevant questions at the end of the interview.

What you must *not* do when answering interview questions:

- Never answer a question if you do not understand it. Obtain clarification first.
- Never say anything negative about previous or present employers, work colleagues, suppliers or customers.
- Never blame others for your shortcomings.

- Never disclose any confidential information relating to current or previous employers. No matter how you are pressed for details simply say that the information is confidential.
- Revealing anything confidential will immediately disqualify you from the running.
- Never give a simple 'yes' or 'no' answer when more information is required.
- Never undervalue yourself or your experiences.
- Never apologise for lack of experience.
- Never reveal anything negative about yourself. If anything is uncovered give mitigating evidence and introduce supporting positive traits.
- Never assume that the interviewer has studied your CV or application form.
- Never interrupt the interviewer, unless absolutely necessary.
- Never jump to conclusions. Let the interviewer finish asking his question.
- Never argue with the interviewer.
- Never talk too much.
- Never look at your watch.
- Never go off on a tangent.
- Never make jokes.
- Never swear or use slang.
- Never discuss other jobs you failed to get.
- Never introduce personal or financial problems into the discussions.
- Never introduce controversial or ethical issues.
- Never appear anxious or desperate to get the job.
- Never lie.
- Never say anything you cannot substantiate.
- Never exaggerate your accomplishments.
- Never become emotional.

Practice makes perfect

A lot of people approach interviews with the belief that they can improvise as required. They think that they will get through if they are just themselves. They decide to 'wing it'. They inevitably crash and burn.

Rehearse your answers in advance. The more you rehearse the better you will get. Rehearsing will enable you to think of better ways of presenting your case. You will gain confidence in advance of the interview. You will become more fluent in your responses during it. You will also become better at side stepping any pitfalls. You will be able to steer the conversation away from your weaknesses and towards your strengths.

Carry out mock interviews

You can arrange to attend mock interviews through school and university careers offices. Older candidates can avail of facilities at job clubs. You can look at recorded mock interviews on career advice websites or simply search on you-tube.

Alternatively you could carry out a mock interview using a friend to ask you the questions you have prepared. Your friend should be able to give you advice on your performance. You could use a web cam to record this session. Play it back later. Analyse the recording for areas in which you could improve. Look out for speech, facial expression and body language. You can even practise in front of a mirror.

All of these actions will help improve your interview performance. If you do not prepare in this manner you will have to use real interviews to gain this experience. This will lead to rejection at the first few interviews. You will make too many basic mistakes. Performance will only improve with practice. Think about the number of driving lessons you took before attempting the actual driving test. Didn't all that preparation and practice pay off in the end?

Getting off to a good start at the interview

First impressions are very persuasive. As soon as you walk into the room the interviewers will begin to form an impression of you. This impression has a disproportionate influence on their decision making. Interviewers tend to remember the first impression you make and the last. The tendency to remember the first things we encounter is known as the primacy effect. The tendency to remember the last thing we encounter is known as the recency effect. Given these effects it is critical to start and finish well.

Get off to a good start by smiling, being polite and maintaining eye contact. Summarise your main selling points into a few short paragraphs. Learn this off in advance. You can develop this from your personal profile in your CV. Use the first available opportunity to introduce this summary of your main selling points. Most interviewers will begin by asking you to tell them a little bit about yourself. This provides the perfect opportunity to sell your strengths and suitability for the role.

Interviewers tend to subconsciously reinforce favourable first impressions it in the early stages of the interview. The interviewer will have a tendency to pay attention to supporting information. He will subconsciously ignore or play down conflicting information.

Understand why you are being asked the question

Every question will be aimed at finding out one of the following points:

- Are you capable of doing the job?
- Are you willing to work hard and achieve results?
- Will you integrate well with colleagues and remain in the role?

These are the three main factors that are used to decide a candidate's suitability. Every time you are asked a question take a moment to consider which of these three factors concerns the interviewer. This will guide you in your answer. You will know which example from your experience will fit best.

Relate to the interviewer's needs

Every company is primarily interested in results. The interviewer will acknowledge your level of responsibility in previous roles. This is not, however, his main concern. He will also recognise your achievements. However your achievements remain with your past employers who have accrued the benefits.

Of paramount importance to the interviewer is your ability to replicate these achievements with his company. He is not interested in what you did. He is interested in how you did it. He wants to know exactly what skill set you possess. What qualities do you have that enabled you to achieve these results? Can you repeat the process with his company?

Consider the needs of the company before answering each question. What exactly does the interviewer want to hear? Which skill set is he referring to? Which example illustrates it best? How should I phrase my answer to show what I can contribute to the company in the role?

Focus on what you can contribute in the advertised role

Spend more time talking about how you can produce results in the new role, than you do describing past achievements. Relate your story to the interviewer's company. He is concerned with his own organisation, not your previous employers.

Too many candidates concentrate on their past experiences. They fail to emphasise what they can bring to the role.

Give practical supporting examples

Do not give general hypothetical answers with meaningless clichés. Every answer should contain practical examples of your experiences and skills. Quantify the benefits you brought to your previous employer. Emphasise what you learned and how you developed. Indicate how you can tackle the issue again, under similar or differing circumstances.

Listen carefully to each question

Listen carefully to each question you are asked. Take your time before responding. Do not give the first answer that occurs to you. Consider your response. Do not make assumptions.

If in any doubt ask for clarification before you begin your answer. Consider the following:

- What exactly am I being asked?
- Why is the question being phrased in this manner?
- What is the interviewer's concern?
- Is he anxious about a particular issue?
- How can I reduce the interviewer's risk and uncertainty?
- How can I help him overcome his doubts and fears?
- Which example from my experience should I give to reassure him?

Pay close attention and concentrate carefully

Keep your concentration levels high throughout the interview. If you are constantly thinking about what you should say next you will not be paying attention. You will miss out on verbal cues and the body signals being given off by the interviewer. You could miss an opening. You could answer a different question to the one you were asked. The interviewer will assume that you were not paying attention. Worse still, the interviewer may think that you are being evasive. He will think that you have something to hide.

Build rapport with the interviewer

It is critical that you build and maintain rapport throughout the interview. If there are several interviewers, find out if the immediate supervisor is present. Concentrate on building rapport with him. Focus on what he is saying. Study his body language. He will have the ultimate hiring decision. He has the vested interest. He must live with the consequences of the selection decision. He must work with the appointed candidate.

Address the interviewer by name. Use his title and surname. Only use his first name if you are invited to do so. Be polite.

Demonstrate that you are actively listening. Agree with the interviewer's views. Echo his values. Demonstrate common interests and outlooks. Smile and humour him where appropriate. Compliment the firm occasionally. Empathise with the interviewer where possible.

You must convince the immediate supervisor that you are the right person for the job. He must believe that you will be enthusiastic, friendly and easy to supervise. The type of person who can take constructive criticism. A reliable and trustworthy employee.

The final selection eventually comes down to two or three candidates. There will be little if anything to choose between them. The final hiring decision hinges on personal chemistry between the interviewer and the candidate. The interviewer will go with a gut feeling. He will opt for the candidate he liked best. This is why it is so important to build good rapport. You need this subconscious decision to swing in your favour. In the final analysis candidates miss out on job offers for personality reasons. They are not rejected because they lack ability.

Remain confident

Adapt a positive attitude from the outset. This will enhance your performance. Trust in yourself. Believe in your ability to secure the job offer. Have confidence that you will be successful in the job. All this belief will become infectious. It will improve your self-confidence and your demeanour. It will show up in your body language. The interviewer will come to believe in you too.

Never doubt your abilities

People are often reluctant to blow their own trumpet. Many people are shy and introspective. If this applies to you, remember you must present your strengths in a confident manner. You must not sell your abilities short.

Do not be hesitant or tentative about your ability. If you doubt your ability your performance will suffer. You will not be able to convince the interviewer that you are the best person for the job. Negative thoughts produce negative results. Interviewers are skilled observers and listeners. They can detect signs of self-doubt in your manner, behaviour or answers. Never set limits on what you can achieve. Never let your inhibitions get in your way. If you really believe in your ability then you are much more likely to succeed.

In order to win you must believe that you can win. If you doubt your ability you will not win. Interviewers pick up on signals of self-doubt. They reject candidates if they detect any signs of it. If you don't believe in yourself than why should they? They are looking to hire someone who they can train quickly to perform a role. They believe that confident individuals will learn quicker and perform better.

Remember that most new employees will receive a period of induction and initial training. Most work colleagues will help a new employee with their initial duties. You should therefore be totally confident in your abilities.

Project enthusiasm

You need to adapt a positive, optimistic and enthusiastic tone throughout the interview. The interviewer is looking to hire a self motivated, hard working employee. Someone who will settle in the role and integrate well with co-workers. A great way to convince him of these two essential criteria is to project enthusiasm.

How we say something can have more influence on people than the actual content. Avoid all negative terms. Do not mention dislikes, things you cannot do, or things you prefer to avoid. Instead inject enthusiasm into the conversation. Talk about your achievements and how they relate to the firm. Use positive, affirmative language.

Treat every question as an opportunity

The interview is your opportunity to let your personality shine. Treat every question as an opportunity to demonstrate:

- Your skills, experience and potential.
- Practical examples from your experiences to back up your claims.
- The savings you brought to your previous employer.
- How you can generate revenue, cut costs or increase productivity.
- How you can improve operations, service levels or quality measures.
- How you can work effectively in a team environment.
- Your ability to motivate and persuade others.
- How you are the best person for the job.
- That you can reassure the interviewer over any remaining doubts.

Match up your skills to all of the criteria

Use your answers to demonstrate that you meet all of the essential criteria and as much of the desirable criteria as possible.

You should know where you clearly meet the job requirements. You will also understand where you are weak in terms of the specified requirements. Pay additional attention to those areas where you have weaknesses. Think of practical examples of transferable skills that you can present to strengthen your case.

Leave a copy of your competency list

You can print copies of your competency list in advance and leave them with the interviewers at the end of the interview. They will already have your CV, which contains details of your main experience and accomplishments. In addition you have now supplied them with a separate list of additional accomplishments. These achievements occurred in all the key areas where the interviewer will score your performance. You cannot fail but make an impression with this approach.

Give similar examples if you need to

Sometimes an interviewer will ask you to give a specific competency based example from your experience. You may not have encountered the exact situation he described. If you can, describe a similar experience which demonstrates your ability to deal with the problem.

Use recent examples from your career where possible

Employers place greater emphasis on your most recent experience. They use the last three to five years of your career as a guide to how well you are likely to perform in the job. Do not give too many examples from your early career. The interviewer is aware that employment practice, regulations and guidelines change with time. He may consider your skills to be at best rusty, or at worse obsolete.

Keep it short and to the point

The interview is a business meeting. It has a definite purpose. The interviewer is in charge of the process. He is working to a tight agenda. When answering the interviewer's questions:

- Keep your answers short and to the point.
- Give complete but concise answers.
- Introduce only relevant, supporting information.
- Do not go off on a tangent.
- Do not talk incessantly.
- Do not introduce any unrelated information.

Know when to stop talking

Aim to make three or four short points in response to each question. This is the limit to what the interviewer will be unable to absorb and remember in one particular answer.

If you talk too much you may inadvertently reveal something negative about yourself. When you have finished giving your answer, just stop talking. Wait for the interviewer to ask another question. Do not worry about the silence that this generates. That is the interviewer's concern. He holds the responsibility for conducting the interview. If he wants more information he will ask for it.

If you have answered a question adequately, it is a mistake to elaborate further. If you have nothing to add, then you should say nothing.

Remain calm and collected

Remain calm and collected throughout the process. Do not be thrown by any unexpected tactics from the interviewer.

Certain disconcerting things can occur during a typical interview. The interviewers will take notes during the process. There may be brief delays while this occurs. Do not be concerned. This is a normal part of the process. The notes will be used to score your performance after the interview. This will be carried out before the next candidate is invited to enter the room.

The interviewer may look at his watch from time to time. This is simply his method of checking that the interview is still on schedule. As long as you restrict your answers to about two minutes each time you should not be concerned.

During the interview you will be asked to elaborate on various points. The interviewer will be looking for additional supporting information. The interviewer may back track to something you said earlier. This is all common practice. It does not usually indicate that you have said anything wrong.

Do not under value yourself

Never, ever, introduce any information about your weak points. Even a minor point might tip the scales against you in the final analysis. There is usually little or nothing to choose between the best two or three candidates. People remember negative information much more readily than positive information. The interviewer will recall negative information when making any final decisions.

Never under value your work experience. Always point out the merits of your accomplishments, even in part time or training roles.

If asked to give your weak points pick a single example of something minor and unrelated to the job requirements. Indicate how you are working to improve it.

Your preparation will have made you aware of your weaknesses in comparison to the job requirements. Do not draw attention to these weaknesses. Always steer the conversation in the direction of your strengths, skills and experience.

Take nothing for granted

Never assume that the interviewer has read and understood your CV or application. Sell each and every one of your relevant skills. Show how they match the core and desirable competencies of the position. The interviewer may have overlooked, or forgotten, some important aspect of your application.

Politely correct the interviewer if he has underestimated the depth of your knowledge or experience in a particular area. He will score you incorrectly if you do not take this action. This may be enough for the job to be offered to someone else.

Look for cues from the interviewer's body language

Always check the interviewer's face for signs of agreement, approval and understanding. These include nodding, smiling or adding agreeable comments. Leaning forward indicates interest.

If you have said something with which the interviewer has a problem you will get a different reaction. He will frown, raise an eyebrow or have a quizzical or surprised look. You need to ask about this and add some clarifying or supporting information.

If the interviewer is behind schedule he may start glancing at his watch. This means that you have given enough information on the current section. Stop talking and wait to be asked the remaining questions.

Towards the end of the interview the interviewer might start stacking papers. He may glance or nod at the other interviewers. This means you are running out of time. It is your last chance to add any final supporting information.

Answering tough questions

Examples of tough questions, including advice on how to answer them is given in Chapter 33. If you are asked a tough, unanticipated question, remain calm. Take your time before answering. If you are not sure what is being asked, then seek further clarification. This will also buy a little time to think. Never try to bluff the interviewer. If you do not understand, or cannot answer a question, it is better to be honest and admit this. This is better than being caught out at bluffing. You can always ask to come back to the question later.

Do not become flustered if you fail to answer a question well. Forget about it. Concentrate on the next question. Do not let it affect the rest of your performance. You can review your performance after the interview. Most candidates will struggle at one or two difficult questions. The important thing is the overall impression you make. You will be judged on how well you can fit in with the organisation and your potential new boss. Personality is every bit as important as the content of what you say. Every question should be treated as an opportunity to highlight your strengths. You still have every chance of being selected. You just need to make fewer mistakes than everyone else.

Interviewers who talk too much

Do not be too concerned if the interviewer has a tendency to talk too much. He will talk too much with the other candidates also.

Just concentrate on presenting your main selling points. Focus on building rapport.

Do not interrupt the interviewer. Allow the interviewer to control the process. If you do, inadvertently, interrupt the interviewer apologise immediately and invite him to continue.
Only interrupt if time is running out and you need to give some relevant supporting information. This type of person does not usually like to be interrupted. In any case, he will fail to unearth any negative information about you while he is talking.

Finishing well

Before you finish you will be given the opportunity to ask questions. There is one question you must ask. This is whether the interviewer has any reservations about hiring you. This will give you one last chance to overcome any objections.

At the end of the interview you should be told what the next stage involves and the likely time scale. If not, do not be afraid to ask for these details.

It is important that you finish well. Interviewers tend to remember your finish due to the recency effect. Finish off by restating your main selling points. Say that you are confident you can do the job. You will contribute quickly in the role. You will work hard and get results. Say that you would enjoy working with the rest of the team. These are the main factors which influence the selection decision.

Thank the interviewer for his time and tell him you are looking forward to his reply. Shake hands with the interviewer before leaving. Do not hang about after the interview. This creates the impression of insecurity.

The false ending

Remain on your guard throughout the complete interview process. Never assume that the interview has ended until you have left the premises. You may be told the interview is over and then be escorted to reception. The interviewer might continue to chat informally on the way to reception. He might ask the odd question. Do not drop your guard. Continue to answer all questions carefully until you have left the building.

Chapter 20. Introductory interview questions

Competency based interviews often begin with a few open ended questions. These can be answered in a wide variety of ways. Interviewers deliberately place no constraints on the candidates. There is no direction on how the questions should be answered.

Use your answers to provide evidence that your work related and personal skills match the specified job requirements. Your answers to the first three questions should demonstrate that you have all of the essential, and most of the desirable criteria.

If you can manage to do this in a concise manner, you will not only give a favourable opening impression, you will be well on your way to securing the job offer.

Tell me a little about yourself.

This is the first question many interviewers ask. It can be disconcerting if you have not prepared an adequate answer in advance. It is a wide open question. It can be answered in a multitude of ways. Your answer must be relevant to the vacancy. You will be judged on how well you relate your experiences to the job requirements. You must be able to do this in a clear, concise manner. The interviewer is also interested in your level of self-awareness.

Keep your answer brief and relevant to the job requirements. Take no longer than two minutes to answer. Do not give your autobiography. If the interviewer wants more detail, he will ask follow up questions.

How you answer this question will set the tone for the whole interview. Use your personal profile from your CV to help construct an answer in advance. Describe your relevant experience, key skills, accomplishments and personal qualities. Give practical examples of your recent achievements. Briefly describe what attracts you to your chosen profession.

Concentrate on your more recent experiences. Quantify the savings or benefits you have achieved for recent employers. Show how you can apply your experience in the advertised job. Emphasise key personal attributes such as your enthusiasm, work commitment, reliability, ability to communicate and team working skills.

Do not talk about your early life, family background or hobbies. Do not go through your CV from start to finish.

What sort of person are you?

The interviewer wants to know which personal attributes you feel will make you successful in the role. He wants to know if you will work hard and be compatible with co-workers and your boss.

Describe your interpersonal skills. Talk about your positive qualities such as honesty, integrity, reliability, flexibility, determination, motivation and positive work ethic. Give actual examples from your work experience. Indicate how they have benefited your previous employer. Show how you have contributed to your existing team. You need to reassure the interviewer that you will work hard, stay committed and get along with fellow employees.

Who do you feel has had the most influence on your life? Why?

The interviewer wants to know which personal attributes are important to you. These need to match the attributes required for the job. The question is aimed at assessing your level of self-awareness. How have you developed through personal growth?

You could give an example of a famous person. However it is better to describe a role model you knew and interacted with personally. This could be a youth leader, sports coach or perhaps a previous boss.

Describe why you were influenced by this person. Why did he inspire you? What interpersonal qualities did this person possess? Perhaps he led by example. He set clear goals and encouraged his team to perform better. He listened attentively, offered a sympathetic ear and empathised with people's problems. He got the best out of each individual. He seemed to know what made people tick. He praised people in public and offered constructive feedback in private. He boosted team morale and supported everyone in their individual goals.

Point out that you have learned a lot by observing how this person interacted with others. You were inspired by the way he continually developed the people around him. He fostered his relationships. He continually encouraged others to achieve their goals. You now try to emulate him every day, in all of your working relationships.

What motivates you?

The employer is looking for self-motivated employees who will work hard, achieve results and encourage others. Employers prefer to hire employees who possess intrinsic motivation. The type of person who completes tasks because of the inherent satisfaction involved. They will avoid employees who rely solely on extrinsic factors to motivate them. Those who only react to external rewards such as pay, praise and promotion before they will apply themselves. This type of employee puts in less effort and achieves less than one who is intrinsically motivated.

The interviewer also wants to know if the environment in which you feel most motivated matches the company's workplace.

Reassure the interviewer that you are self-motivated. You work hard, achieve results and integrate well with others. You are motivated by intrinsic factors such as:

- Satisfaction in a job well done.
- Solving challenging problems.
- A sense of achievement.

- Responsibility.
- The opportunity to make a difference.
- The chance to improve your skills.
- Serving your customers.
- Helping others.
- Personal growth.

Incorporate the key skills required for the job in your answer.

Don't answer that you are motivated by extrinsic factors such as money or rewards. This implies that you are only interested in yourself and have not considered the employer's needs.

You must show enthusiasm when talking about what motivates you. This will sound more convincing and credible.

Tell me about the following topical issue ......

This type of question is favoured in graduate recruitment interviews. You are not being tested on your knowledge of the subject. The interviewer is just interested in your ability to debate a topic. Can you weigh up the available evidence and come to a rational conclusion? These common skills are required in every work environment.

It is difficult to anticipate the likely question. Read and watch news items in the days before the interview. Look out for issues related to the industry. You may be asked about general business issues such as economics, inflation or taxation. You will not be asked about politics, war or religion.

If you do not know a great deal about the topic, keep your answer brief. The interviewer will simply use another question to test your reasoning and problem solving abilities.

Chapter 21. Questions on your education

If you have a lot of work experience the interviewer will not dwell on your education. Your work experience is more relevant. He will concentrate on that area instead.

If you are at the early stages of your career, more emphasis will be placed on your education. You will be asked about subjects you enjoyed and those in which you did not perform well.

The interviewer will equate academic grades to potential future job performance. Your results should indicate that you are motivated, enthusiastic, self-disciplined and hard working. Did you work unaided? Did you meet assignment or project deadlines? Did you overcome difficulties and setbacks? Did you work well as part of a team? These are all skills that can be replicated in the workplace. What academic skills did you acquire? Can you apply them in the workplace? These are the issues that concern the interviewer.

Which were your best subjects? Why?

Be prepared to talk about your best academic subjects. Explain that you worked hard at all subjects. However you performed better in some because you had a natural disposition for those subjects. Do not say that you worked harder because you liked the subject. You will be assigned certain tasks at work which you do not like. However you will be expected to complete all tasks to the same high standard.

Do not say that you did well because you liked the teacher. This implies that you will reserve your efforts at work for bosses you like. You could say that the teacher was better at explaining things.

What subjects were you least good at? Why?

Do not say that you did not like a weaker subject. This implies that you will only produce results at work when assigned tasks you like. Do not say anything negative about the topic or your experiences. This reinforces the perception that you only apply yourself to tasks you like. Do not blame the teacher for poor results. This implies that you will blame others at work to cover up for your own lack of commitment and results.

Point out that you worked harder at weaker subjects to try and improve your results. You can say that you got extra assistance or coaching. This displays a willingness to persist when faced with adversity. At work you will be assigned some difficult tasks. The important thing is to persevere and seek assistance if required.

What subjects did you like most at school? Why?

The interviewer wants to see if you only worked hard at subjects you liked. What motivates you to perform well?

Talk enthusiastically about your favourite subjects. Think of some sensible reasons for enjoying them. For example you might have liked history because it helped you understand people and societies and how the world evolved. You liked geography because it helped explain the physical systems that affect everyday life.

Point out any practical, numerical, written, artistic, linguistic or mechanical skills you acquired. Show how these could benefit your performance in the job.

What subjects did you least like at school? Why?

The interviewer wants to know that you worked just as hard at subjects you disliked as those you preferred.

This is a difficult question to answer. Pick a subject that you dropped at school. You can say that it did not fit into your plans. Otherwise, give a subject in which you got a reasonable grade. Say that you worked just as hard at it as the subjects you liked. This will show that you will persevere at work, even with tasks you don't like.

Why did you choose those subjects?

The interviewer is looking to see if you had a fixed career destination in mind. Did you choose your subjects as part of your career plans? Or did you just end up where you are by chance? Candidates with a defined career path are more likely to settle in the job. They are less likely to leave at the first available opportunity in a different industry.

Relate your chosen subjects to your final career choice. For example you chose to study mathematics as a route to mechanical engineering at university before becoming a design engineer. If your chosen subjects are unrelated to the vacancy, then just say that you wanted to keep your options open. You will need to give a convincing argument for seeking this particular job. You must convince the interviewer of your long term commitment to your current career.

Why did you choose your college or university?

The interviewer wants to know that you took such a career and life defining choice seriously. If so, you are likely to take your job and career choices seriously. This will strengthen your case for selection.

Answer that you chose your university for its reputation in your given subject. Do not say that you chose it because it was nearby. Indicate how you came to a logical decision in your choice of university. You first studied the prospectus of several universities. You then talked to your school's career advisor. You studied the UCAS and various university websites. You visited your short listed choices to get a feel for each place. You spoke to some current undergraduates from your college or school. Finally you came to an informed choice.

Show that you followed a detailed, rational thought process before making a decision that would affect your career and life. This indicates that you will not rush into accepting a job that is unsuitable for you. You are more likely to stay if you accept a job offer.

Describe a special project you carried out at school or university.

Can you relate any skills you acquired while undertaking projects to the job requirements?

Talk about the skills you acquired while doing any background research. Show how you collated, analysed, summarised and interpreted the data. Explain how you prepared and wrote any reports. Talk about the practical skills and experience you gained from placements in industry. Describe how you worked effectively in a team environment. Show how you met deadlines.

Talk about any computer systems you used. Give your level of proficiency. Describe the communication skills you acquired while preparing and giving presentations. Mention any merits or awards. Think about what you got out of the project work. Relate this to the employer's needs. Show how you can apply the skills you acquired in the advertised role.

What did you gain from your time at school or university? How has your education prepared you for your career?

The interviewer will expect you to summarise experiences and skills that can be applied in the job. College or university education presents great opportunities. Did you make the most of these opportunities?

This is a great opportunity to sell your personal skills. This is a wide open question. You can list loads of examples.

- You matured and developed independence.
- You met new friends and made professional contacts.
- You developed your interpersonal and communication skills.
- You balanced your studies and outside interests.
- You managed your time.
- You managed to budget your income.

- You prioritised your work.
- You developed self-discipline.
- You met deadlines.
- You coped with the pressure of exams.
- You worked independently while carrying out research.
- You acquired team working skills working in group projects.
- You gave presentations.
- You developed your language skills.
- You improved your computer skills.
- Your good grades indicate that you are motivated and work hard to get results.

Do not mention any regrets or negative comments about opportunities missed. Do not say that you could have achieved more.

Do you think you performed better or worse than you expected at school?

This question is not actually about your performance. The interviewer wants to know how you estimate your own ability. If your results were worse than expected, you may tend to overestimate your ability. Most people do. He will be wary of your claims in the balance of the interview.

If your results were better than expected you may have low self-esteem. You may lack the confidence level required to deal with certain work related tasks.

Answer that you did as well as you expected. Alternatively, say that you did better than you expected in some subjects and worse in others.

You don't seem to have done so well at school. Why is that?

This is a difficult question to answer, especially if you are just starting out on your career. Past achievement is taken as the best indicator of future performance. If you have not performed well in your education, what guarantee does the interviewer have that you will suddenly apply yourself at work?

Give any genuine reasons you have for not performing well. Maybe you had problems with your health. Perhaps you were the main carer for a dependent parent. You might have had to work long hours to fund your studies.

If you have no valid excuses for your poor results then just say that you have since matured. You now regret not working harder at school. Point out any qualifications you have acquired since leaving school. Detail any current studies you are undertaking. Explain that you were focused on gaining employment experience at the time.

How did you spend your vacations?

Point out any work experience you gained during your vacations. Indicate the skills you acquired. Link these skills to the specified job requirements. If they are not directly related, then emphasise transferable skills. Examples might include dealing with customers, handling cash, selling product or meeting deadlines.

If you lack vacation work experience, then say you spent time in active hobbies or interests. Outline the skills you acquired. Show how these can be applied to the job.

Chapter 22. Questions about leisure interests

You will not be asked about leisure interests if you have a lot of work related experience. If you have little or no work experience interviewers will concentrate on your education and may ask some questions on your leisure interests.

Interviewers ask about leisure interests to help get a rounded picture of the candidate. They are interested in what motivates you. Why did you take up the hobby? What relationships did you develop? Any leisure related achievements could indicate future potential.

You can use questions about your interests to overcome any possible unspoken reservations about your age. So if you are young for instance you can point to positions of responsibility. If you are over 50, you can talk about activities requiring physical stamina.

If the interviewer shares your hobby then acknowledge this. However do not get drawn into an extended conversation. You have a limited time available. You need to spend it answering job related questions in more detail.

If you are applying for an internal promotion you are unlikely to be asked about leisure interests. The company has sufficient knowledge of each candidate's work experience on which to make a decision.

What do you like to do in your spare time?

Talk enthusiastically about your interests. Explain your level of participation in clubs, societies or competitive teams. Talk about any positions of responsibility. Describe briefly what you have contributed. Mention any skills you acquired. Talk about any voluntary work.

Show how any skills you acquired could benefit the employer. Examples include communication skills, teamwork and organising skills. Include any practical experience such as maintenance, woodworking or DIY skills. Include only genuine interests in your application. You need to be able to talk knowledgeably on the subject.

Which is your main leisure interest?

Give a brief description of your main interest. Pick something in which you are proficient and knowledgeable. Point out the hard work you put in, your level of proficiency and the goals you achieved. Talk about your dedication and commitment. Give examples of any team activities and positions of responsibility. Dedicating several years to a particular club or society shows commitment, discipline and integrity. Talk about the skills you developed. Show how you can apply these in the work environment.

The interviewer will only probe if he shares the hobby or he thinks that you are not being genuine in your response. He may, for example, be suspicious if you know little about a sport, despite claiming to have held a position of responsibility.

How much time do you devote to your main interest? How proficient are you?

Be careful how you answer this question. Remember that the interviewer expects work commitments to come first. Employers are reluctant to grant employees time off to attend competitions or events. Point out that your sport or hobby will be arranged to suit the demands of the job.

Committing a lot of time to a sport or hobby demonstrates many desirable qualities. Examples include dedication, discipline, integrity, team work, goal setting and perseverance when things have gone wrong.

If you are not proficient at sports or hobbies just point out that the demands of family and work have always come first. Your sport, or leisure interest, gave you a chance to unwind and keep fit. It provided an opportunity to interact socially with your friends.

What do you get out your hobby or interest?

The interviewer is interested in what motivates you and how you interact with others. What you get out of any activity is invariably related to what you put in.

Talk about the satisfaction you gained from your achievements and responsibilities. You welcomed the opportunity to develop new skills. You enjoyed socialising with others and the chance to contribute to team success. Your hobby gave a welcome break from the demands of your daily routine. It gave you a chance to unwind and relax. It helped provide a healthy work-life balance.

Have you held any positions of responsibility in clubs, societies or voluntary groups?

Give details of any current or previous positions of responsibility such as club chairman or secretary. Mention if you volunteered or were elected to the role. Describe what you learned from the experience. Examples could be participating in meetings, organising and promoting events, getting investment and negotiating contracts. Perhaps you were involved in preparing documents, giving presentations or communicating with club members and the public. You may have developed leadership and motivational skills by coaching junior teams. Show how this could benefit your performance in the job.

If you have not held any positions of responsibility, just point out that the demands of family and work were much more important.

What is your favourite type of reading? Why?

Your reading habits indicate your interests.

It is better to say that you read factual material rather than fiction as it increases general knowledge. You could answer that you read management books or books related to your profession. Alternatively, say that you read self-improvement books such as time management or leadership books to enhance your career prospects. You could say that you read biographies of successful entrepreneurs or famous people. This gives you inspiration and ideas that you can apply in your own career.

Do you watch much television? What type of programmes do you prefer? Why?

Do not say that you watch a lot of television. This will suggest that you lack motivation. You need to stress active hobbies or interests.

Relate any viewing to your profession and hobbies. If you are applying for a nursing job say you watch programs on the NHS. If you are looking for a technical job say you enjoy DIY programs. If applying for a journalist or media role you would say you study news and current affairs programmes.

Chapter 23. Questions about the company

If you are really want the job you will have done more than the minimum research on the company. If you have failed to do this, you will be rejected as being uninterested in the position.

Why do you want to work for this company?

The interviewer wants reassurance that you are genuinely interested in working his company. Will you settle in and work well with colleagues? Do you understand what it would be like to work for the company? Is working for this company your preferred choice? What are your real motives? Are you running away from problems elsewhere?

Answer the question you were asked. Concentrate on why you want to work for the company. Do not talk about what attracts you to the job itself.

Valid reasons for wanting to work for the company include a good reputation for:

- Employee relations.
- Working conditions.
- Quality of products and services.
- Safety.
- Innovation or research and development.

If the firm is expanding or diversifying into new regions you could give this as an answer.

Explain how the working environment will help you to develop new skills and experiences. You are looking forward to taking on extra responsibility and contributing to the success of the firm.

Never quote pay and conditions as a reason for applying. Never mention the desire to leave your current job as the motivating factor.

What do you know about our company?

The interviewer wants to know if you are genuinely interested in working for the company. Have you done more than the minimum of research? Do you appreciate the ethos of the company? Have you considered what it would be like to work for the company?

Describe your knowledge of the firm. Talk about its background, products, number of employees, structure, locations, market position, customers, suppliers and competitors. Give the name of the CEO or managing director.

Talk about the company's mission statement. Its ethos or culture. Make sure your information is current. Mention any recent news stories relating to the company. Compliment the firm. Say that you are keen to work for them. Explain your reasons for wanting to work for the company.

Never, ever say anything negative about the company. Never refer to any negative press they may have received.

What do you think of this organisation?

Praise the company. Say that you have heard it is a great place to work. Quote some positive aspects of the firm. Examples include good employee relations or reputation for quality and safety. You will find suitable information on the company website. Talk enthusiastically about the prospects of working for such a good employer. Make it clear that you would like to develop with the company and take on extra responsibility.

What are our main products and services?

The interviewer wants to know that you have done more than the minimum of research. The depth of your research will indicate your real interest in the job. Certain jobs in product development or sales require detailed knowledge of products and services.

Make sure you can list a range of products or services. Give additional information such as new products under development. Indicate how the company advertises and markets its products. During your research get hold of and study product catalogues, sales brochures or specifications. Quoting additional information from these will set you apart from other candidates.

Who are our main competitors?

The interviewer wants to know if you are genuinely interested in the industry. How aware are you of commercial competition?

Give details of two or three main competitors, including their main products. Indicate what differentiates their offering. Compare the company with its competitors in terms of size, products, marketing tactics or pricing policies.

Stress what attracts you to the company as opposed to its competitors. Do not say that the company is worse than its competitors in any way.

How would you rate us against our competitors?

The interviewer is checking your knowledge of the company and the competition.
Is the company your preferred employer?

You must rate the company favourably against the competition. Explain how the company is your first choice as the best place to work.

Study company sales or product brochures as part of your background research. Sales brochures promote the main selling points of a company's products. They also indicate marketing strategy and what differentiates their products from the competition. Quote this information to the interviewer.

The company website will emphasise positive aspects of the company in terms of market share, growth, innovation or research and development facilities. Incorporate these points into your answer.

Who is the head of our organisation?

You should be able to provide the proper name, title and position. Include a couple of very brief sentences on his background and employment history. This will set you apart from the other candidates.

In which part of our organisation are you most interested? Why?

Graduates applying to larger organisations are often asked this question. These companies offer graduates an extended training period in several departments. Once they are trained, there is an option to specialise in a particular area.

The extent and location of the vacancies varies from year to year, depending on prevailing circumstances. A common mistake is to focus on an area where vacancies do not currently exist. The company may be contracting in the specified area. You may, unwittingly, exclude yourself from the process.

First ask where the current vacancies are concentrated. Then pick the most obvious area where you have some experience or qualifications. Outline your experience and say what attracts you to this area. Explain how it fits in with your long term career plans. Emphasise what you hope to contribute. Explain how you intend to develop your skills with the company.

Do you know anyone working for the firm?

If you do know someone working for the company arrange to meet them before the interview. Ask them about the company. Ask about the job and department to which you are applying. This helps you understand what it would be like to work for the company. Tell this employee that you are really keen to join the company.

Volunteer this person's name, job and department when asked this question. The interviewer might ask them for their opinion on you. This will be after the interview, but before they make any final selection decision. That person will say that they met you recently. They will probably say that you asked a lot of pertinent questions and you seemed very keen to get the position. This will boost your chances of being short listed.

Chapter 24. Questions about the job

When talking about the prospects of doing the job you must sound enthusiastic. You need to have done your homework on the job. You must clearly understand what it entails. You need to demonstrate that you can do the job. You must demonstrate that you will work hard. You must convince the interviewer that you will fit in with the existing team.

Why have you applied for this job?

The interviewer wants to know if you fully appreciate the job requirements. Are you confident in your ability? Are you committed to being successful in the job? Will you fit in? The interviewer will reject any candidate who is not genuinely interested in the job. They will avoid anyone likely to treat the job as a stop gap while looking for a better offer elsewhere.

Use your answer to illustrate not only why you have applied, but why you are the best matching candidate. Acceptable reasons for wishing to apply include gaining more experience, developing your skills or improving your chances of promotion.

Convey interest and enthusiasm when talking about the prospects of doing the job. Show that you have thought about the job and the implications of taking up the position. You fully appreciate what is needed to succeed in the job. Highlight your relevant qualifications, skills, experience and attributes. Show how the job fits in with your career path. Give examples of how you have achieved results in similar roles. Indicate what you can bring to the job. Show how you can contribute as part of the team.

Focus on the attractions of the job and not the reasons you wish to leave your current position. Never mention difficulties in your current job as the motivating factor for moving on. Never give convenience to your home or attractive pay and conditions as a reason for applying.

What is your understanding of the job?

Job titles can often be misleading. Have you researched the job? The interviewer is checking that you fully appreciate the responsibility level of the job. For example the level of budgetary control, number of employees you will be supervising and decision making authority.

Explain how the job fits into the organisation. Demonstrate that you fully appreciate the responsibilities, accountabilities, and competencies required. You understand the main tasks to be carried out and the scope of the role. Indicate in each case how your own experience matches the specified job requirements.

What skills do you think are required in the job?

Use your answer to indicate that you understand the skill level required and also to demonstrate that your level of proficiency.

Start with the essential criteria as listed in the advertisement. Give brief practical examples of what you have achieved in recent roles. Demonstrate the benefits you could bring to the role. Then move on to the desirable criteria. The more matching experience you can quote the better.

Finish by listing your personal attributes that can be utilised in the role. Examples include dedication, leadership or interpersonal skills. Show how your strengths would help you contribute to the success of the team.

How would you approach this job?

Can you make a contribution after a reasonable period of induction? Will you integrate well with the existing team?

Consider the job requirements from the company's perspective. What do they want in terms of results? What are their key performance indicators? How do they expect someone in this role to behave? Incorporate these factors into your answer.

Explain that you would begin by acquainting yourself with the job and personnel. You would discuss targets and priorities with your new boss. You would agree a plan of action. You would set short, medium and long term goals. You would regularly review your progress against these targets. You would help the existing team to succeed by working hard and meeting targets and deadlines.

You would make suggestions for improvements, based on your experience of how things were carried out more efficiently with previous employers.

How would you change things if we were to hire you?

Be tactful when answering this question. The company wants someone who will fit in with their existing ways of doing things. Nobody appreciates a heavy handed, know it all attitude, particularly in a new employee. Someone, on day one, informing experienced staff that they have being doing things wrong for years. There are usually valid reasons for doing things a certain way. This is not obvious on a cursory inspection. Bear in mind that the line manager may have developed the existing methods. Having said this, companies do like to make savings. They constantly seek to improve working methods and procedures.

Answer that you would spend your induction period assessing the people and systems. This will help you appreciate how the job integrates with other departments. Having grasped company procedures and policies you would look at areas requiring fine tuning.

Ask the interviewer which areas he feels need tackling first. Then give examples of how you have tackled similar problems under comparable conditions. Indicate how you have reduced costs, improved efficiencies or developed better results. Say that you are confident you could replicate this in the new role.

Only deviate from this answer if you are aware that that they are seeking someone to introduce rapid and dramatic cutbacks.

What challenges do you expect in this position?

The employer wants to hire someone who will be motivated, work hard, meet deadlines and achieve results.

This is an opportunity to show what you can contribute to the role. Speak enthusiastically about the challenges you will face. Say that you would expect to face similar problems to those that occurred in your last job. Then explain how you overcame challenges in your current or previous roles. Show how the lessons learned can be applied in this role. Use your answer to show how you have held an equivalent level of responsibility. Indicate how closely your experience and skills match the criteria.

Chapter 25. Questions about your work experience and achievements.

Unless you are a school leaver, or recent graduate, the interviewer will place most emphasis on your work experience. Recent work experience will be deemed more relevant. Recount as many achievements from the last five years as possible.

The interviewer will be looking to establish the depth of your skills and experience. What was your level of motivation? Did you overcome obstacles and persist when facing adversity? Did you show initiative, commitment, drive and enthusiasm? Can you meet deadlines, introduce change and support team members to achieve common goals? Demonstrate how you have gone beyond the basic job requirements in previous roles to bring real value to your employers.

What have been your main achievements in your current job?

The interviewer wants to know if you have been proactive in your current role. Have you introduced any changes to improve current operations? Or have you simply carried out your duties as described in your job description?

Relate your achievements to the advertised job requirements. Give specific examples. Quantify your achievements in terms of reduced costs, improved efficiency, increased revenue, or improved quality or safety. Show how you persisted to overcome difficulties, instigate change and achieve results. Demonstrate that you can achieve similar results in the advertised role.

Describe your greatest achievement to date?

The interviewer is interested in the competencies you developed, such as planning, organising and decision making skills. How can you apply these skills to the advertised job?

Pick a major project that is fairly recent. One in which you made a significant contribution. Highlight the challenge. Show how you:

- Analysed the problem.
- Considered the alternatives solutions.
- Evaluated the risks involved.
- Decided on the time frame.
- Set goals and deadlines.
- Prioritised and delegated tasks.
- Consulted with interested parties.
- Kept your boss informed.
- Proposed the optimum solution.
- Made your final decision.
- Implemented the proposed solution.

Stress your personal involvement. It is better if you were the instigator. Quantify the benefits that accrued to your employer. This might include efficiency savings or improvements in sales, quality or safety. Indicate what you learned from the process. Explain how you can bring similar gains to your new employer.

What has been the greatest problem you have had to overcome?

The interviewer wants to gauge your competency level. Can you handle the responsibility level required in the role? Can you achieve results? Can you sort out problems yourself? Or do you continually need to refer them to your boss? The employer wants someone who will get on with the job. Someone who can devise and implement solutions. The use of the word 'problem' is deliberate. It is set as a trap for those who might divulge relationship issues.

Pick a relevant practical example that is linked to the job requirements. Talk about a particularly difficult project where you had to meet a tight deadline. Perhaps you were low on resources. Show how you managed to meet targets by organizing, planning, communicating and setting clear objectives. You delegated tasks and enlisted help where you could. Perhaps you had to postpone all other non essential tasks for a few days to get the job done.

Show how you contributed positively within the team and supported others to get the job done on time and within budget. Outline what you learned from the experience. Indicate how you improved methods to avoid the problem recurring.

Make sure you do not talk about a problem that you caused. Do not talk about problems with work colleagues.

What problems did you encounter in your current job?

Be careful. This is an open invite to reveal negative information that would cause you to be rejected. The interviewer is looking for evidence that you persevere and overcome problems. What have you learned from your experience? What procedures have you introduced to avoid the problems recurring?

You should sound upbeat and talk about a challenge rather than a problem. Describe how you analysed the issues and listed any probable solutions. You evaluated the implications of each before selecting the optimum solution. Explain that you kept your boss informed of progress at each stage. Outline the benefits that accrued to the company in terms of savings or efficiency improvements. Talk about what you learned from the experience. Show how you can apply this knowledge in the new role.

Do not mention any problems with your performance. Do not talk about relationship problems with your boss, work colleagues or customers. Do not talk negatively about the job itself or any problems you encountered.

What has been your greatest failure? What has been your greatest mistake?

This question is used to eliminate candidates who reveal major failings in their character or actions.

The interviewer wants to know how you cope with major problems or setbacks and how you resolve them. Do you learn from your experiences? Do you take precautions to prevent a recurrence? Everyone makes mistakes, but not everyone learns from them.

Do not fall into the trap of admitting to a major mistake or failure. This will cast doubt on your ability to succeed in the job. As far as you are concerned you have not made any major mistakes. Instead give an example of a medium level set back. Perhaps a problem with the timing of a project.

Explain what you did to rectify the problem. Pick something from your early career.
Ideally something affected by circumstances beyond your control. For example a cancellation by a major customer. Something that involved the complete team. This way everyone failed rather than you individually. Show how you resolved the problem. Indicate what you learned from the problem. Explain how you ensured that it would not occur again.

Never blame anyone else for your failures. Never admit to covering up a problem.

What do you like best about your current job?

The interviewer wants to know that the aspects you enjoy in your current role are an integral part of the advertised job.

Remember to sound enthusiastic when talking about your current or previous jobs. Say that you take pride in your work. You enjoy many aspects of your current job. Pick some skills required in the advertised job. Say that your current job gives you an excellent chance to exercise these skills. You enjoy being able to contribute to the company's success. You welcome challenges. Say that you enjoy working with colleagues.

Do not volunteer any information about your dislikes at work unless you are specifically asked this question.

What do you like least about your current job?

The interviewer wants to know if you will evade chores you dislike.

Do not express a dislike for chores that are an essential requirement in the advertised role. You will not be short listed. The interviewer will conclude that you would not be happy in the role.

Do not say anything negative about your current, or previous, employers or work colleagues. Do not give the impression that you are unhappy in your work.

Say that you enjoy all aspects of your job. You are very happy in the challenging environment. Then pick something outside of your control which inhibits the performance of yourself and your team. Perhaps you dislike red tape that delays project or investment approval. However you understand the need for effective policies and procedures. Keep any criticism constructive and balanced and show an appreciation of the company needs.

Why are you looking to leave your current job?

The interviewer wants to know if you are serious about getting this job. Are you merely checking out the possibilities? Are you running away from problems elsewhere? Do the same issues exist in the advertised role?

Never say anything negative about your current boss, employer or work colleagues. Criticising your current boss in any way will ensure that you are automatically rejected.
Do not reveal other relationship problems in your current role. Do not say that you want to leave because you failed to get a promotion. Do not say you fancy a change. Do not say that you want to leave for personal reasons. The interviewer will assume that there is a conflict between you and your boss. Perhaps you have issues taking instructions.

Focus on the attractions of the new role. Give positive reasons why you are applying for the job. Acceptable answers are promotion, broadening your experience, more challenge, better pay and conditions, more security, or better prospects.

You may be asked why you left several previous employers. Do not say you left for better pay each time. This implies that you will leave at the first sign of a better offer elsewhere.

Do not get drawn into a lengthy explanation for leaving a job. It will sound like an excuse and that you are covering something up.

What did you get out of your current job?

You get out of a job what you put in. What effort did you put into your last job?

Do not just say job satisfaction. Point out the relevant skills you developed and the contributions you made. Remember to sound enthusiastic. Give examples of your dedication and work ethic. Show how you enjoyed working with colleagues. Talk about the things you learned. Describe any transferable skills such as leadership, communication, problem solving and organising skills. Show how you can apply these skills to the advertised job.

Do you think you have been successful in your current job?

The interviewer is looking for signs of self-doubt in your abilities. He is trying to gauge your self-esteem. If you have any doubts in your ability, then why should he want to hire you?

Do not confess to any doubts whatsoever about your ability. Show confidence in how you performed in your current job. This is not a time to be modest. Say that you would definitely consider yourself very successful in the role. Talk about any good performance reviews you received. If you have been promoted then point this out. Perhaps you have taken on additional duties.

Detail any improvements you made in terms of quality, safety, efficiency, cost or productivity. Talk about how the skills you developed will enable you to repeat the savings in the advertised role.

Did you think your progress in your current job reflects your abilities?

The interviewer is looking to gauge your level of self-worth. He is also looking to uncover any problems with authority. Promotion is linked to individual effort and performance rather than just ability.

Point out any promotions, increases in responsibility and temporary upgrading. Be careful not to blame others for any lack of progress. You can say that opportunities for advancement were limited due to budget constraints. Point out that you continually analyse your performance in order to learn from your mistakes and improve your contribution to the firm. You listen to any advice your boss offers during performance appraisals. You continue to work hard and be proactive. This is why you are applying for this role.

How do you try to improve your performance at work?

Say that you always take advice from your boss. You listen to ideas from more experienced colleagues. Say that you regularly review and analyse your performance to develop better ways of doing things. You read management and self-improvement books. You volunteer for additional duties to broaden your experience. You attend training courses in agreement with your boss. You keep short, medium and long term personal goals. You regularly review your progress against each. You work hard, utilise your time effectively and learn from your mistakes.

What skills do you need in your current job?

Quote the essential skills required for the vacancy. Give examples of how you have used these skills to achieve quantifiable benefits to your current employer. If your current job is unrelated, then quote transferable skills that match the job requirements. Show how you can apply these skills in the new role.

Why were you made redundant?

Redundancy is a common occurrence. You do not need to be concerned if asked this question. Keep your answer simple and short. Point out that the job became redundant and that is why you were let go. If you were the victim of last in first out agreements then just point this out. Also point out if you were retained longer than other employees because of good performance.

Have you had much computer experience?

Employers prefer to hire people with computer skills. It is becoming a prerequisite in many jobs. Technology levels are constantly expanding. Computers are being used in more jobs, including shop floor applications. You will be expected to have some computer experience, particularly for office jobs. There is a wide demand for word processing and spreadsheet skills. Many employers expect you to be able to use e-mail.

State your level of proficiency in any applications you have used. If you lack computing skills you should enrol on a short course. These are usually available at a modest cost through local technical colleges.

Chapter 26. Questions about decision making skills

Time is money. Employers expect their staff to be able to make effective decisions in a timely manner. They do not want people who procrastinate, sit on fences and abdicate responsibility. Decisions often need to be made in situations where the problem is complex and the outcome is uncertain. This requires judgement which comes with experience.

Interviewers will look for evidence that candidates carry out a systematic approach when making major decisions.

Which decisions do you find most difficult to make?

Can you can make tough decisions and follow through on them without procrastinating unduly? The interviewer will reject candidates with an aversion to certain problems or situations, such as having to discipline subordinates.

This is a common behavioural question. Give a specific example of a difficult work related decision that you have had to make. Explain why you found the decision difficult. The problem may have been complex or the risks high. Alternatively the outcome may have had an emotional impact on yourself or others. Show that you did not shirk your responsibilities. You followed the important stages of any decision making process by:

- Analysing the problem.
- Considering the alternatives.
- Evaluating the risks involved.
- Narrowing the viable options.
- Consulting with everyone involved.
- Taking advice from your boss.
- Reviewing what worked in the past.
- Proposing an optimum solution.
- Making the decision.
- Implementing the proposed solution.

- Reviewing the situation in terms of the lessons learned from the experience.

How do you make important decisions?

The interviewer will avoid hiring anyone who rushes into hasty decisions. Someone who selects the first alternative that occurs to them. Someone who does not consider the options and the likely implications to themselves and others. Someone who does not consult with their boss or more experienced colleagues before taking action on important decisions.

Give a practical example from your experience. Show how you followed the decision making process as given in the answer to the previous question.

After making a decision do you stick to it?

The employer does not want you to become entrenched in a position that is not generating results. They do not want you to cover up problems. They want you to adapt to changing circumstances.

Answer that you are confident in your decisions and the likely outcome. However circumstances change. After implementing any change of procedure you check that the outcome is beneficial as anticipated. You monitor the situation over a representative period of time under various conditions. Sometimes the results are not as expected. This might be due to other changes that have occurred since the solution was implemented.

If this is the case you consider your options. You propose corrective action. You keep your boss informed. You analyse any probable causes so that you can learn from the experience. You update procedures to benefit the company.

How do you decide on your objectives?

Answer that you review your overall objectives periodically with your boss. You then draw up a short, medium and long term plan. Urgent objectives with immediate deadlines are included in your short term plan. You also include things that can be completed quickly, but which will reap significant benefit. Medium term objectives are those that take more time and need more resources committed to them. Your longer term objectives tend to be personal objectives such as gaining more qualifications or acquiring new skills.

Within each plan you prioritise your goals. You ensure that these are specific, measurable, achievable, realistic and deliverable. As you complete each objective you take another step towards your long term goals.

You set realistic time frame for each objective. You set targets to reach by a given time. You break larger targets down into smaller more achievable steps. You monitor your progress at each stage. You take corrective action if required. You review and update the plan periodically with your boss.

Are you willing to take risks?

Risk is defined as deciding on a course of action where there is a possibility of failure. The interviewer wants to know if you are willing to take initiative. Can you make rational decisions? Do you take short cuts? Reckless behaviour can affect the company in terms of profits and reputation. However commercial success depends on a certain amount or risk taking. Companies usually have to speculate to accumulate.

Your answer to this question depends on the job to which you are applying. In certain jobs, such as civil service work, it might be frowned upon if you take risks. You are expected to rigidly adhere to procedures and guidelines. In this case you need to answer that you avoid taking risks. You take great care and are never reckless. You like to identify potential risks in advance. You take corrective action to avoid them. You report and potential risks to your superiors.

In other careers, such as investment banking, calculated risk taking is the norm. In this case you would answer that you regularly take calculated risks, within recognised parameters. You realise that not all risks are equal. You do not take unnecessary risks. You only take calculated risks after carefully considering the benefits versus the possible losses. You only proceed if the potential benefits far outweigh the possible losses. You always reduce the exposure to the risk by spreading it if possible. You regularly re-evaluate risks as circumstance change. You do not take risks if the situation is irreversible. If in any doubt you always check with your boss. There is no substitute for experience.

There is a difference between taking a risk and taking a short cut. Never give examples where you have taken risks with the safety of yourself or others or the reputation of the company.

Chapter 27. Questions about time management skills

Employers expect their employees to use their time effectively. They expect them to organise their work in order to prioritise important issues and meet deadlines. They will reject candidates who waste time and interfere with the efficiency of others.

How do you prioritise your work load?

Point out that you prioritise your workload in agreement with your boss. Say that you keep a list of short and medium term priorities. You update the short term priority list at the beginning of each day. Medium term priorities are updated at the end of each week.

You always prioritise the most urgent and important jobs to be carried out first. You delegate as much routine work as possible. You check on the results regularly. If the workload becomes excessive, you consult your boss. You ensure that all tasks are carried out on time. This way performance does not suffer.

How would you manage your time in a typical day?

You could say that you keep a list of outstanding tasks. You update this at the beginning of each day. You prioritise any new and outstanding tasks in terms of importance and urgency. You begin by reviewing any new e-mails and correspondence. You check any voice-mail. You reply to these as necessary and note any further action required. You then update your to-do list and calendar as appropriate.

You look at the priority tasks and work out if there is enough time to complete them all. If not you get help from colleagues or let your boss know that there are resourcing issues. At the end of the day you like to leave an hour free to complete any urgent tasks. You also use this time to review what you have achieved and how you might have done things better.

Tell us about a time management skill you apply to your work.

Any of the following examples would be acceptable:

- Setting clear goals and prioritising tasks.
- Planning and scheduling your work effectively.
- Breaking larger tasks down into smaller, more manageable tasks.
- Delegating as much work as possible.
- Re-routing calls to avoid distraction and interruptions.
- Making timely decisions.
- Managing your emails and paperwork.
- Managing your boundaries.

You regularly challenge the processes and methods used. You like to streamline by getting rid of any redundant or unnecessary paperwork or procedures.

What kind of things do you prefer to delegate?

Knowing how to delegate makes managers more productive. It frees them up to concentrate on medium and longer term strategy. The interviewer will also probe to see if you tend to avoid difficult tasks or situations.

Answer that you delegate as much as possible based on the level of responsibility required. You particularly like to delegate:

- Anything you don't need to do yourself.
- Anything for which you are overqualified.
- Anything that someone else can do faster, cheaper or better.
- Routine or repetitive tasks.
- Specialist tasks to the appropriate experts in your, or other, departments.

You let people get on with the tasks without interfering unnecessarily. You check on the work when it is completed or at agreed intervals. Your team knows that you are available if they encounter a problem needing your assistance. As your people become more skilled and experienced you delegate more challenging tasks and let them get on with it.

Chapter 28. Questions about your personality and character

Interviewers are looking to hire candidates who will be motivated, hard working, committed, dedicated, honest, enthusiastic and willing to learn. The type of person who is proactive and will persevere and achieve results, regardless of setbacks. Someone with integrity who shows a positive outlook.

What are your greatest strengths?

The interviewer is interested in your key selling points? How do these relate to the job? He also wants to gauge your level of self-esteem.

This is an ideal opportunity to sell your suitability for the role. Talk about those personal attributes that are required to be successful in the job. Avoid vague, unsubstantiated, terms. Saying that you get on well with people or work well in a team environment is not good enough.

Give specific examples of how your strengths have benefited your current employer. Quantify your achievements in terms of the savings or improvements you made. Show how you can replicate these savings for your new employer.

Qualities to stress include:

- Willingness to work hard and exceed targets.
- A proactive approach.
- Positive attitude.
- Interpersonal skills.
- Time management skills.
- Energy and enthusiasm.
- Dedication.
- Reliability.
- Flexibility.

- Integrity.
- Ability to learn.
- Communication, especially ability to listen.
- Team working.

Be careful not to appear to be arrogant when talking about your strengths. You should select three or four items from this list. You will have opportunities in later questions to cover your other strengths.

If you are weak in any core competencies, then use this opportunity to stress transferable skills.

What are your weak points?

The interviewer is trying to unearth any weaknesses that could prevent you from carrying out the job to the required standard. He also wants to gauge your level of self-awareness. Are you aware of your weaknesses? Do you review your performance and work to improve on it? If so, you have potential for future growth. You should not think that you are perfect.

Answer this question as briefly as possible. Give only one example of a weakness. Make sure the weakness is not related to the specified competencies for the vacancy. Never pick anything major or irreversible. Pick something minor. Explain how you are working to overcome the weakness. Show that it does not hamper your work performance. Describe how your behaviour is changing. Explain what you have learned from the experience. Say that you do not have any weaknesses that would prevent you from excelling in the job.

Some people select something that can also be regarded as strength. A common example is over attention to detail. Another example is impatience when poor commitment from others or red tape delays progress. A favoured answer is reluctance to delegate work because results may not meet your own high standards. Do not use this example if applying for a supervisory or management role.

Never admit to any serious weak points. Never own up to doing anything foolish or selfish. Never admit to taking short cuts with procedures or safety. Never admit to breaking company rules or procedures. Never blame anyone else for your shortcomings.

Never deny having any weaknesses. The interviewer will not accept this answer. Everyone has some weaknesses. If you do not recognise your weaknesses you are either arrogant or lack self-awareness. The interviewer will assume that you have not analysed previous job performance. The interviewer will not hire anyone who denies responsibility for their own shortcomings. He will opt for someone who has learned from their mistakes and gained valuable experience.

Do you think you are good with detail?

The interviewer wants to be assured that you are hard working, committed, persistent and determined. Do you stick to the task? Do you complete tasks to the necessary standards?

How you answer this question depends on the level of responsibility in the role.

You may be asked this question if you are expected to complete tasks on your own.
Answer that you take pride in your work. You are meticulous, thorough and exact. You like to see that tasks are completed to the correct standard. You always double check critical items.

Alternatively you may be applying for a management position. In this case answer that you set the work priorities and assign the tasks. You leave others to complete the details. You appreciate that it is critical to ensure that the detail is correct. However you must delegate the work and trust and support your team. You would check on the results at agreed intervals, paying close attention to critical factors. You encourage your team to report problems or difficulties to you. If they are not sure of their results they always check with you.

Do you work well under pressure?

Pressure is present in the workplace because of the need to meet deadlines. Missed deadlines can lead to penalty fines, dissatisfied customers, lost reputation and cancelled orders. Employees are expected to take the appropriate actions to meet deadlines. This might involve putting in additional effort or working overtime. The interviewer will reject anyone who is unwilling to work hard or take on additional responsibility. So your answer should be a definite yes.

Give an example of a situation where you achieved results on time and to specification despite being under resourced. Show how you remained calm, analysed the issues and set priorities. Outline how you met targets by delaying non essential tasks, enlisting help and encouraging other team members to put in additional effort.

Let the interviewer know that you enjoy a challenge. You can mention that your current job has a certain amount of pressure. However be careful. Do not say that you are constantly under pressure. The interviewer will assume that you cannot manage your time properly, or delegate responsibility.

Do you think the only way to get a job done properly is to do it yourself?

If you are applying to a supervisory role you will be expected to delegate work. You will be overqualified for many of the tasks. Quite often others are more capable of doing the job than you are.

Individuals are often expected to take full responsibility for completing individual tasks. However tasks are also regularly shared within a group. Often one group will begin a task, while another group will complete it. This occurs, for instance, when processing accounts.

The answer to this question is no. You are quite happy to complete all tasks assigned to you. You take pride in the quality of your work. You always check your results. However, it is not in the interests of the company to have only one person qualified to do a job effectively. It is better to have back up in the event of you being committed to some other activity. This is a more flexible arrangement for the company.

What have you have learned from your mistakes?

Everyone makes mistakes, so don't deny making any. Answer that you have learned quite a lot from your mistakes. Learning is a process of trial and error. Scientists and researchers often eliminate what will not work before finding solutions. Everyone makes mistakes, especially when tackling an unfamiliar problem. This is the nature of progress and innovation. A certain level of risk is needed if worthwhile results are to be obtained.

You could say that you regularly analyse your performance at the end of each day. This way you learn from your mistakes and avoid making them twice. This is how you continually gain new experience. It enables you to work out new ways of tackling problems. The lessons learned help you to avoid making serious or costly mistakes. You regularly review any issues with your boss. You never cover up your mistakes, or blame them on someone else.

Some common things to learn from mistakes:

- Double check critical factors and results.
- Seek assistance when required.
- Get advice from more experienced colleagues.
- Keep your boss informed.
- Persist despite initial setbacks.
- Consider all the options before making decisions.
- Listen more carefully to instructions.
- Listen to feedback.
- Delegate more.
- Do not jump to conclusions.

Do not give any examples of having made serious mistakes. Do not give the impression that you regularly make mistakes. Do not give examples of other employees discovering mistakes that you have made and over looked.

How do you cope with stress?

People suffer from stress due to an adverse reaction to excessive pressures placed on them. Stress occurs when the level of pressure exceeds your capability to meet the demands placed on you. Stress reduces an employee's effectiveness and can lead to absence from work due to the effects on health. Some people are more susceptible to stress than others.

The interviewer would rather hire someone who:

- Is robust and can cope with stress.
- Recognises the early signs of stress in themselves and others.
- Appreciates how it can adversely affect their performance and health.
- Takes appropriate action to reduce stress levels.
- Can cope with the demands of a busy and challenging workplace.

The interviewer will avoid anyone who suffers from stress and folds under pressure. The type of person who is likely to take time off work due to stress related illness. Pressure is present to differing degrees in every job. Employers can work to minimise pressure, but they cannot eliminate it. It is a fact of life.

Remain positive and upbeat when talking about work pressures and stress. Begin your answer by pointing out that you work well and thrive under pressure. However you recognise the difference between a healthy challenge and overload. Give an example from your experience where you completed a difficult project on time despite tight deadlines and scarce resources.

Say that you recognise the early symptoms of stress in yourself and you take corrective action. You minimise the degree of stress in your work. You do this by organising your workload and workplace. You manage your time effectively. You set priorities and delegate where possible. You enlist the help of colleagues. You make decisions promptly. You avoid unnecessary conflict with colleagues. When the workload surges due to unforeseen or emergency situations you keep your boss informed. You discuss methods of reallocating or re-prioritising the workload. You delay work that is not urgent.

Explain that you use one of the common methods of relieving stress. These include exercise or practising a relaxing hobby. Many people like to unload by talking to a friend and seeking advice. Never say that you take a drink to unwind after work or enjoy a smoke as a method of relaxing.

How do you respond to change?

Every company survives by reacting to changes in demand. They do this by developing new products and methods of trading. Companies who welcome and embrace change are the most likely to succeed. Employers need their employees to be flexible to change. They want to be able to alter employee duties, working patterns and workloads depending on demand.

Say that you are flexible and welcome change. You continually acquire new skills and adapt to circumstances. You welcome change as an opportunity to improve working methods and efficiencies. Demonstrate that you do not simply react to change. You are proactive in bringing change about. Give an example of how you have promoted and implemented change in your current role.

Give an example of a time when you were proactive.

Proactive employees initiate change in advance of anticipated circumstances. This saves time and money. They do not wait and react to events after they have occurred. They recognise and correct negative trends or situations that are likely to have an adverse effect on performance. The interviewer wants to know that you show some form of initiative. You do more than the minimum required to get the job done.

You need to explain that you continually show initiative and like to be proactive. You like to monitor how things are progressing. You regularly look at results. You check on feedback from customers. You look at discrepancies. You question how things are done. If results are trending in the wrong direction, or anything looks out of place, you consider the issues. You review the problem with interested parties. You look at all the suggestions and feedback. You propose a course of action and discuss it with your boss. You implement the solution.

Give an example from your experience where your proactive approach saved the company from possible losses.

Chapter 29. Questions about interpersonal skills

Interpersonal skills are very important to employers. They want to hire people who will fit in with work colleagues and contribute to the success of the team. They are looking for people who will be enthusiastic, confident, dedicated, hard working, motivated, agreeable and easy to get on with. They will avoid hiring anyone who is likely to be disruptive to others.

Remember when talking about teamwork to focus on the goals of the team. Mention the importance of everyone's contribution to the end results.

Would you prefer to work as a member of a team or would you rather work alone?

Most jobs require their employees to have clear specific areas of responsibility, but also to work as part of a team.

The best answer is therefore to say that you feel equally comfortable working in either role. You believe that teamwork is essential in the work place. Every individual team member has their own specific role to play. However everyone must cooperate to get the job done. Team members have different skills and are assigned different tasks. It is how they integrate that leads to the desired successful outcome. Unless everyone pulls his weight, the team will not achieve its goals.

You enjoy completing your individual assignments. You are happy to assist the team in its goals. You are very comfortable working with others and like to help out when you can.

If the interviewer forces you to pick one option or the other then opt for the one most likely to be required by the job.

Can you describe your management style? How do you manage your staff?

Expect to be asked this question if applying for a management or supervisory role. The interviewer will avoid anyone who is overly autocratic and also anyone who is too laissez faire. Can you influence others to meet targets? Can you handle people diplomatically?

Say that you are a leader who tries to get the best out of his team by:

- Setting clear objectives and communicating these to the team.
- Allocating tasks according to ability.
- Letting people know exactly what you expect from them.
- Treating everyone equally, fairly and objectively.
- Setting realistic targets.
- Providing the best available resources.
- Trusting your team to get on with it.
- Checking progress at agreed intervals.
- Encouraging and praising effort publicly.
- Listening to feedback and concerns.
- Offering advice when required.
- Pointing out privately when someone does not meet your targets.
- Giving credit to the team.
- Providing a mechanism to allow your people to develop.
- Accepting responsibility for problems.

You like to develop good working relationships with all of your staff. You maintain an open door policy. You carry out regular performance appraisals. You support and encourage your staff to improve their skills and take on more responsibility.

Would you rather be liked or feared?

You may be asked this question if applying for a management role. The correct answer is neither. If you are feared your management style is too authoritarian. People will be afraid to approach you with problems and may prefer to cover them up. If you are liked you may not have set the correct boundaries. You will be viewed as lacking assertiveness and being unwilling to discipline subordinates.

The correct answer is you would rather be respected.

How do you get things done?

The interviewer is interested in how you plan and organise your work in order to achieve your objectives. How do you interact with others and get them to work for you?

A good answer is that you draw up lists of what needs to be done. You then prioritise the work according to importance and urgency. You review this list daily. You tackle urgent tasks first. You then complete anything that will derive the most benefit in the immediate term. You delegate what you can, according to skills required and the balancing of workloads. Stress that you clearly define the allocated tasks and get subordinates to regularly report on progress. You instigate contingency plans in cases of unforeseen events. You check with your boss regularly to ensure that your priorities coincide with his.

How do you motivate others?

The interviewer wants some indication of your interpersonal skills. He wants to know how you interact with others.

In the short term you praise employees who are doing a good job. You encourage everyone to try and do their best. You try to make the job more rewarding. You do this by giving your team greater responsibility and control over the process. You set realistic targets with a degree of challenge. You avoid overloading your staff. You encourage your team to make suggestions. You act on these whenever possible. You listen to their concerns. You provide the best resources available. You try to lead by example.

You promote the right people. You make sure that those employees who contribute most are given the long term rewards in terms of promotion, bonuses or better pay.

Are you sensitive to criticism? Tell me about a time your previous boss had to criticise your work?

This is another question primarily aiming to uncover weaknesses. The added difficulty this time is that the work is probably related to the tasks in the advertised position.

The interviewer will reject anyone who cannot accept constructive criticism. The type of person who likes to place the blame elsewhere. It is counterproductive for the individual and the company if someone holds a grudge against his boss for criticism received. The interviewer does not want to employ a difficult, over sensitive employee. Your prospective boss will need to criticise your performance occasionally. He does not want someone who will make the experience unpleasant for him.

Therefore the simple answer is no, you are not sensitive to criticism. You are a mature individual. You understand the need for employers to provide feedback on performance.

You recognise and accept that criticism is a form of advice to help you improve your performance. It is directed towards your actions and not yourself as a person. You remain rational and react positively to criticism. You take time to think about the other person's perspective. You ask for clarification. You learn from any feedback you receive. You think about your actions and how they affect the overall performance of the team. All criticism is an opportunity to improve future performance.

You understand that sometimes criticism will be brief and to the point and not necessarily phrased in the most constructive manner. This can occur due to the pressures of the working environment. If this happens you just get on with things. You usually find that your boss will explain things more fully when things have settled down.

Point out that your boss usually is very positive about your work performance and has seldom had reasons to question the quality of your work. Then give an example of a minor isolated issue that arose and show how you took on board the criticism and improved the standard of your work from there onwards. Highlight what you have learned from the experience.

Are you a competitive person?

Employers require a workplace that is conducive to getting things done efficiently, in a harmonious atmosphere. Workers who are over competitive can create disharmony in the workplace. The working environment requires team work. Companies value collaboration.

Your answer should be that you are a competitive person. You are, however, not overly competitive. You understand the importance of cooperating with others to achieve common goals. You do not try to gain recognition at the expense of the team. You assist others as required. You share information and pass on your knowledge and experience to others. This helps to get the best possible outcome for the team.

Explain that you understand that everyone must work together. Different team members have their own particular skill set. It is a combination of these that makes the team successful. Similarly all departments must co-operate to meet overall company goals.

What kind of people would you find it difficult working with?

This is a loaded question. The aim is to unearth relationship problems that would exclude you from the process. Are you obstinate and argumentative? Do you make bad situations worse by clashing with difficult co-workers? Are you prejudiced against any particular groups? Do you respect differences in others? Can you behave with tact and diplomacy? Can you deal constructively with awkward situations and difficult colleagues?

Do not to be critical of others for personal reasons. Say that you generally get on well with everyone at work. You seek to understand differences in others. However you minimise your contact with people who are continually complaining or gossiping.

The type of person who gets involved in office politics. You do not like to be associated with this type of behaviour. These types of people do not have the best interests of the firm at heart.

How did you get on with colleagues in your previous job?

The interviewee is looking for any signs of relationship problems. Any hint of a problem will be enough to exclude you from the process.

Never admit to relationship problems with work colleagues in a previous job. It does not matter how you describe the situation and your lack of blame. You will have cast doubt on your ability to work in a harmonious atmosphere with co-workers.

Answer that you got on well with everyone. You enjoyed working in a team environment. You developed a good working relationship with all of your colleagues.

Give an example of how you helped a colleague with a work related or personal problem. Perhaps you participated with colleagues in external clubs or activities? Talk about a time you all got together to organise an event for charity.

How would your colleagues describe you?

The employer is trying to gauge your interpersonal skills. Will you fit in with the existing team? Your answer will indicate how you perceive yourself and how you think others perceive you.

You could answer this in a number of ways depending on your personality. First you could say that colleagues often share their problems or issues with you. They come to you for advice. They would describe you as friendly, loyal, empathetic, a good listener, honest and caring. They know you will help out in any way you can.

Alternatively if this does not fit in with your personality traits you could answer in a different way. You could say that colleagues would regard you as someone who takes initiative and comes up with ideas. Or possibly someone who works hard, plans ahead, perseveres and encourages others to meet goals.

Give an actual example of how you helped out a colleague to support your claims.

How do you contribute to your team?

Team working skills are very important to employers. The interviewer is looking for someone who integrates well with others. Someone who listens to and appreciates the views of others. Someone who can communicate. Someone who contributes to group tasks. Do you understand your role and the contribution expected of you?

Think about the requirements of the role. What is your expected input for the team? If you are applying for a supervisory role then concentrate on leadership qualities. If the role is a technical one, you will be expected to offer technical advice and develop the ideas of others.

Summarise your interpersonal skills in a few sentences. A typical answer would be that you enjoy working with others and like to contribute to results. You actively participate in meetings. You contribute ideas and seek solutions. You keep the group focused. You actively support and encourage the input of others. You organise the workload and priorities. You are flexible and willing to help others in order to meet deadlines.

You could contribute specialist knowledge. Perhaps you help resolve disputes. Some people like to ensure that everything is completed correctly.

Describe a situation where you were confronted with conflict from another employee?

Employers prefer to hire someone who can avoid unnecessary conflict. The type of employee who can diffuse emotions and focus minds on the task at hand. Someone who gets on well with others.

However they do expect you to be assertive if required. You should be capable of diplomatically defending yourself and your department when dealing with someone who is being unreasonable.

Point out that you rarely get into conflict situations. Then give a specific example of a problem you encountered and how you overcame it. Do not complain about the person or people with whom you had the conflict. It is important to show that you:

- Remained calm and professional throughout.
- Used a common sense approach based on facts not emotions.
- Communicated clearly your point of view.
- Listened to the other person's views and remained open minded.
- Respected the viewpoint of the other person.
- Were fair in your dealings with this person.
- Tried to reach accommodation if possible.
- Kept your boss involved at every stage.
- Reviewed your behaviour later to see if you could have handled it differently.
- Have learned from the situation.

Explain that you dealt with any problems with individuals privately.

Give me an example of a time when you had to deal with an irate customer. Explain how you handled the situation.

You will be asked this question if you are applying for a customer services or retail sales position. Your ability to handle unhappy and angry customers is very important to the firm. The company does not want to lose the customer's business. Unhappy customers pass on news of their negative experiences to other current and potential customers.

Give an example of how you have previously dealt with a difficult customer. Outline how you listened carefully to the customer's complaint. You explained to the customer that you fully understood and sympathised with their problem. You promised that you would do everything you could to rectify the situation as quickly as possible. Perhaps you did not necessarily agree with the customer. However you attempted to regain the customer's trust as soon as possible. If the customer was right you apologised on behalf of the company.

You advised the customer of their rights. You offered a refund or exchange goods or compensation within the company policy. If you were unable to give the customer what they wanted you offered an alternative. Describe what you did to rectify the problem and satisfy the customer.

Demonstrate that you remained calm, professional and diplomatic. You empathised with the customer while remaining solution focused.

It is best to give an example where the customer's problem was resolved. A good example is one in which you went beyond your normal job duties in order to obtain a solution. You left the customer more satisfied with the company than before the issue arose.

You might be asked how you would react if the customer refused to calm down and accept your offer of compensation. The answer is that you would refer the customer to your boss. Customers feel vindicated by being able to take a problem to the next level to get reassurance that it will not recur.

How would you rate your customer service skills?

You obviously rate them highly. Point out that you have good listening skills. You empathise with your customers. You keep in contact with your main or regular customers. You are polite and professional. You smile when talking to them. You ask if they need any help. You listen to their concerns. You keep them informed of new products and services. You inform them about upcoming promotions or events. You take pride in resolving customer problems as soon as possible. You respond to any concerns in writing.

Give an example of how you dealt with a difficult customer to their satisfaction.

What makes you lose your temper?

This is a loaded question. Losing your temper is a sign of immaturity and a lack of tolerance. It means you have lost control of the situation. You are making a bad situation worse by aggravating others. No one wants to hire an employee who will upset colleagues by insulting or inappropriate behaviour such as shouting or cursing.

Answer that you never lose your temper at work. You are even tempered. You deal with people in a professional manner. You do not provoke anyone at work.

If you are confronted in an unprofessional manner, you focus on remaining calm. You always find a middle ground. You concentrate on the problem, not the personalities. You quickly steer the conversation onto the issue that needs resolved and away from any emotions.

If someone tries to draw you into confrontation you like to take a quick break from the situation for a few minutes to calm down. If this is not possible you count to ten before you continue.

Give an example of a time when you had to deal with a difficult subordinate?

The interviewer wants to know if you have the leadership skills to deal with difficult employees. The important thing to point out is that you don't ignore the problem.
If an employee's behaviour is inappropriate it will be counterproductive and adverse to the goals and morale of the team.

Problems do not resolve themselves. By doing nothing you help to reinforce negative behaviour and perpetuate the problem.

You should say that you intervene as soon as possible. Give an example of a time when you had to caution a subordinate because of poor behaviour. You spoke to the person in private. You would never humiliate anyone in public. You remained calm, objective, non confrontational and professional. You pointed out the area of his behaviour which did not meet the required company standards. You clearly explained what these standards were. You point out the negative effect the behaviour is having on the rest of the team. You helped the employee view their behaviour from the perspective of others. You listened carefully to the employee's viewpoint and took it into account if there were any mitigating circumstances. You outlined what he needed to do to improve his performance.

You agreed a period of time for the performance to improve. You reviewed the progress at specified intervals.

It is important to point out that you treat all subordinates fairly, equally and objectively,
regardless of their ability or performance.

Chapter 30. Questions to determine your views on authority

Any sign that you have difficulties with authority or taking criticism will be enough to cause you to be immediately eliminated from the process.

How would you rate your current boss?

The interviewer wants to find out if you have any problems with authority. Would you be likely to criticise him to other employees or managers if you were his subordinate?

Do not say anything negative about your boss. No recriminations, no back biting, no bitterness, no grudges, no hinting at any problems whatsoever in your working relationship. Even if the interviewer insists and says there must have been an occasion when you did not see eye to eye you still should refuse to divulge any relationship issues. If you do, you are out of the running. You might as well terminate the interview there and then.

It is best to answer that you have a good working relationship with your boss. You agreed your targets with your boss in advance. You kept him regularly updated on your progress. You discussed any difficulties, or obstacles to progress, such as resourcing difficulties. You took his advice on these issues. You valued his experience. You would rate him highly.

Tell me about a time you disagreed with your boss.

This question is used to unearth possible relationship issues with your boss. Have you got problems with authority? Can you follow orders without being difficult and obstinate? Can you deal with differences of opinion tactfully?

First of all answer that you seldom disagree with your boss. You value his experience and his insight.

Then pick a minor situation. Show that you took your concerns directly to your boss without consulting anyone else. You did not air your opinions in public or disagree with your boss in front of others. You pointed out your objections privately. You proposed a different course of action and gave your reasons. You explained that you had his interests and the company's interests at the forefront of your reasoning. You asked for his opinions and you listened to his reasoning. If you were wrong you acknowledged this.

If your boss insisted in his original course of action you supported him. You acknowledged his greater experience. You recognised that the responsibility for obtaining results was his. You got on with your job.

How do you think your current boss would rate your work? Can you tell me about your last appraisal?

The interviewer knows that overall appraisals may be balanced in terms of your strengths and weaknesses. However the actual written details in appraisals tend to focus on areas requiring improvement. If you are attending an internal interview he will probably have already read your last appraisal.

Prepare for this question by considering your last performance review. Then list the required core and desirable competencies. Include as many of the good points from your review that match the job requirements. You can point out any positive remarks or scores in previous appraisals. Do not claim strengths that are likely to be contradicted when the interviewer phones for a reference from previous employers.

Quantify what you have achieved. If you have been promoted or received a performance related rise include this in your answer. Point out any occasions where you deputised for your boss.

What would your current boss say are your weaknesses?

This is an indirect method of uncovering your weaknesses. Also the interviewer is probing for relationship problems with your current boss.

Even though the question asks about weaknesses, plural, give an example of only a single minor weakness. Do not select a weakness related to the core competencies for the job.

Your current boss should have carried out some appraisals of your performance. Give an example of something minor from a recent appraisal. Explain that you have an agreed plan with your boss to work on improving your performance. Give an update showing that you are improving. Detail any additional training or study you are undertaking. Say that you regularly review your progress with your boss, who is now happy with your performance in this area.

Chapter 31. Questions to determine your flexibility

You may need to demonstrate flexibility to the demands of the job in terms of relocation, working pattern, hours of work and willingness to travel.

Would you be willing to move to a different part of the country if required?

If you are applying for a job in sales, marketing or senior management you should have anticipated this question. Your answer will have to be yes. Many larger companies have sites across the country. They provide trainees with work experience at various sites as part of their initial training. After this period, employees tend to be allocated a job in their local area. So you will have to accept this initial disruption in order to get the job you want.

Sometimes a firm may simply be asking this question as a precaution. There may actually be little likelihood of you having to move.

Would you be prepared to travel around a lot?

If you are expected to travel in the role then again your answer needs to be yes. Travelling comes automatically with jobs is sales, marketing or senior management. If you are not prepared to travel, you will not be short listed.

Would you be willing to work irregular hours or overtime?

Hourly paid employees are often asked this question. Overtime is used to cover absenteeism and cope with fluctuations in demand. However with most companies the bulk of the overtime is actually worked by a minority of employees. These employees are keen to earn the extra cash. Other people never volunteer to work overtime. They value their time off. However most companies still specify that willingness to work irregular hours and overtime is a requirement for the job.

If you answer no to this question you will not be short listed. If you are keen on overtime then let the interviewer know. If you are not keen on overtime, just reassure the employer that you are flexible. Say that you are willing to occasionally work overtime if it is essential to meet deadlines and targets. Add that you would obviously provide cover for emergency situations.

This flexibility will be enough to satisfy the interviewer. There are enough other people in the workplace willing to work plenty of overtime. Do not ask about payment for overtime or time in lieu. This is provided in most cases. It will be explained if you receive a job offer.

If you were offered a position, when could you start?

If you are currently employed, then give the details of your notice agreement. Otherwise say you can start as soon as required. This question is often asked of all candidates. It does not mean that you will be offered the job. Do not relax and drop your guard.

Do not talk about any plans to take a holiday between your last job and this one. If you get a job offer you can negotiate at that stage. If you need a few days to arrange relocation for a job in a different region this should be acceptable.

Chapter 32. Questions to determine your suitability

Questions on suitability are key to your ability to secure the job offer. They are directly related to one of the interviewer's three main concerns. Will you fit in and be happy in the role?

The main reason that employers give applicants for not offering them the job is that they were not deemed to be the best fit. In other words the company believed that they were not best suited for the job. By implication, someone else was a better fit.

When you are asked a question on suitability you must go all out to persuade the interviewer that you would be very happy in the role. He must believe that you would have a long term commitment to the job and to the company.

Why have you chosen this particular career path?

This question is often asked of people in the early stages of their career. How much motivation do you show towards your career? Are you genuinely interested in this career path and by implication this job? If so you are deemed to be more likely to settle in the job. You are less likely to leave for opportunities in a different career.

Do not give the impression that you just drifted into this type of work. Give a definite reason. Demonstrate that you have been interested in this type of work for some time.
Your initial interest in this career path may have been the fact that it is a profession. Perhaps it is a demanding and rewarding environment. Maybe you have been attracted by promotion prospects or job security. Maybe the career is beneficial to humanity. Whatever your reason you need to project enthusiasm when talking about your motivation for following this career path.

Use your answer to show that you have the right skills for the job. You need to demonstrate that you have a long term commitment to this career choice. Keep your answer as relevant to the company and advertised position as possible.

Do you have any regrets? Would you change anything about your life or career?

The interviewer wants to know if you are content with your chosen career path. He is also looking for signs of emotional problems. Perhaps you regret some of your choices along the way. Any signs that you doubt your chosen path will cause him to believe that you will be unhappy in the job. You will not contribute as much as a contented employee would. There is a risk that you will leave for a different type of job offering more satisfaction. So if you want to be selected for the next stage you have no regrets whatsoever.

You need to give the impression that you are a happy, contented, well adjusted individual. You are happy in your chosen line of work. You have a long term career goal and are working towards it.

The only exception to this answer is if you are switching careers.

Are you confident in your ability to handle this position?

The interviewer is looking to uncover any doubts you have about your abilities. After all, if you doubt your ability, then why should he believe in you?

You just need to be positive and convincing and say that you are very confident in your ability. You have all the necessary skills, qualifications and experience. You have carried out most or all of the required functions in your previous roles. Above all you have the right attitude which will help you achieve success in the job.

You might be asked this question by a personnel manager at a screening interview who needs reassurance about your technical qualifications. Just let him know that you would have no problems whatsoever with the duties. Explain that you have all the skills and personal attributes. You just need to become familiar with any policies and procedures and get to know the rest of the team. You will begin to make a significant contribution immediately upon completion of this period of induction.

Why should we offer you the job? Why do you think that you are suitable for this job?

The interviewer wants to know why he should choose you before all the other candidates. What is your unique selling point?

Stake your claim for being hired. Answer that you believe that you are an ideal match for the specified job requirements. Remember that the interviewer does not want the best candidate. He wants the best match. He does not want someone who is overqualified and hence will not settle in. Nor does he want someone who is under qualified and who will struggle to succeed.

The employer is looking for a smooth transition from the last incumbent to his replacement. Indicate that:

- You can do the job.
- You need minimum or no training.
- You can take on the responsibility of the role as quickly as possible.
- You will fit in with the existing team.
- You will be happy in the role.
- You are self-motivated, dedicated and passionate about your work.
- You will work hard.
- You are organised.
- You will meet deadlines.
- You will achieve results.
- You will be an asset to the company.
- You can take orders or work independently as required.

Highlight your skills, strengths and experience in a similar role. Show that you have all the core essential competencies and most or all of the additional desirable skills.

Convince the interviewer that you are professional, hard working, reliable, enthusiastic and likeable. Display confidence in your abilities. Show enthusiasm at the prospect of joining the company.

Why makes you think that you are better than the other candidates?

In most cases you will not have met the other candidates. The only exception is for internal vacancies or at assessment centres. So just say that you have not met the other candidates and so cannot comment on them. Do not get into a situation where you are criticising others in any way.

Simply answer that you believe you are a very close match to their requirements. Treat the question as if you were asked why the company should offer you the job. Answer the question as advised above.

In which sort of environment do you work best?

The interviewer wants to know if you will be comfortable in the job. Will you get on with other employees? Will you settle in and perform well in their specific work environment?

This is a difficult question to answer. You know little of their working environment. You know nothing about the personalities of the existing team. Do not be specific in your response. You may be describing the wrong working conditions. This will exclude you as being unsuitable for their specific environment.

Keep your answer as broad as possible. Do not show a preference for a particular management style. You do not know how your potential boss likes to get things done. If you have worked in several jobs, just point out that you felt comfortable in all of them. You worked well with different bosses. Give examples of working as part of a team as well as on your own. Emphasise your flexibility and ability to respond to changing circumstances. Point out that you get on well with people. Give examples of where you have taken on extra responsibility or been promoted.

Avoid specific personal demands such as having your own office. Do not give the impression that you may be difficult or demanding employee.

So keep your answer general yet neutral. Say that you are extremely confident that you will get on well in the role. You will quickly make a worthwhile contribution.

Where do you see yourself in five years time?

The interviewer is seeking to hire someone with future potential growth. Have you got a clear realistic career path mapped out in your mind? Are you committed to staying with their firm? He will expect a return on any investment. Are your ambitions realistic? He will reject anyone who is clearly delusional or overambitious.

Remember the company is recruiting for a specific job. They want someone who will commit to the job for a reasonable time period. You must display a rational level of ambition. One step up the career ladder would be a realistic target. Do not appear overambitious. This type of employee can be disruptive in the job, or leave at the earliest opportunity. Instead, show that you are focused and goal orientated. You are dedicated and professional in outlook. You are committed to the company.

Everyone will answer that they want promotion. However that is presumptuous. Differentiate yourself from the other candidates by pointing out that you will need to earn the promotion. You will do this by working hard, taking on additional responsibilities and producing results.

Talk about your aspirations for personal growth. Explain that you are continually learning and developing new and existing skills. You do each task to the very best of your abilities and learn as much as you can. You are quite sure that the company will provide opportunities for employees with the right attitude.

Do not answer that you want the interviewer's job. They have heard that line a thousand times.

What do you want out of a job?

The interviewer is trying to ascertain how close this position is to your ideal job. Will you be comfortable working for the company? What is it that motivates you?

Do not talk about what the job can do for you in terms of pay and conditions. Do not simply answer that you are looking for job satisfaction. Everyone else will give this answer.

Acceptable answers could be additional responsibility or a sense of achievement. Say that you want a challenge. The chance to solve problems and the opportunity to participate as part of the team. The chance to make a worthwhile contribution. You want to know that you have done your best. You would also welcome the opportunity to learn and increase your skills and experience.

What kind of things would you want to avoid in a job?

You need to be very careful when answering this question. The company will not hire anyone likely to shirk responsibility. You must be willing to tackle all aspects of the job enthusiastically. So do not give any work related tasks as part of your response.

Say that you prefer to avoid anything that interrupts with the efficient operation of the job. Examples could be unnecessary conflict or office politics. You prefer to get on with the job and tend to avoid people who spend their time gossiping about others. You do not get into conflict as you understand the importance of a harmonious working environment.

What kind of things would attract you to a job?

The interviewer is trying to see if you will be happy in the role. Are the tasks you enjoy present in this job? If not, you are unlikely to stay for any length of time.

Answer that you would be very happy in the job for which you are applying. You need to be enthusiastic in your response. Give specific reasons. Point out that you were motivated and happy in the past in very similar roles.

You are attracted by the chance to use your skills. You would look forward to contributing to the team. You are looking for a challenge. You want to make a worthwhile contribution.

Was this job your first choice?

The interviewer wants to know if you are serious in your desire to work for the company. Will you remain for a reasonable period of time? He does not want to hire anyone who will leave the moment a better opportunity presents itself.

So do not give the impression that you are applying to a large number of organisations or a wide diversity of roles. You can admit to looking for work with a small number of similar firms. However, stress that this job is your clear first choice.

Give a valid reason for this job being your favoured choice. You could compliment the firm on their employee relations or their training program. Say that your skills match the job requirements. Give practical examples to justify why this is so.

What other types of positions are you applying for?

Undergraduates are often asked this question at milk round interviews. If you are asked this question it means that the interviewer wants to know if you are genuinely interested in the job and the industry. Do you have a clearly defined career plan? Or are you applying for every possible advertised vacancy? If you got the job would you simply be biding your time until a better position became available?

Say that you are applying for a small number of similar roles in the same industry. If you are applying to a broad range of vacancies keep this information to yourself. The interviewer will assume that you have not yet discovered your chosen career path.

Never admit to having been rejected for other positions. This may influence the interviewer's decision. He will fear that other interviewers have unearthed something he has missed.

What would be your ideal job?

The interviewer wants to know if you will be happy in the role if you were hired. So your description of an ideal job should be related to the advertised role. The question is also aimed at unearthing any unrealistic views you might possess of your abilities. So don't tell them you want to be CEO any time soon.

The question is deliberately phrased to tempt you to talk about personal gratification. Do not fall into this trap. Do not talk about what an ideal job can give you in terms of earnings, esteem, status, glamour, satisfaction or other personal benefits.

Most people answer that they would like a job that utilises their main interests or hobbies. This is the wrong answer to give, as it is unrelated to the vacancy. It does not further your chances of being selected.

Do not say that the job you are applying for is your ideal job. This shows no ambition to further yourself beyond the role.

Say that your ideal job is one that is a few levels up from the advertised job. Point out that you realise that you will have to work hard, achieve results and gain more experience, before reaching this goal. This might take quite some time. In the meantime you are committed to obtaining the job for which you are applying.

This question may also be asked if the interviewer feels that you are overqualified and may be treating this job as a stop gap. If you feel that you fall into this category, you should stress your desire to contribute to the role for which you are applying.

What will you do if you do not get this job?

Do not panic if you are asked this question. It does not mean that you will be rejected. There are three reasons for asking this question. First the interviewer is checking to see if you would apply for similar work. This confirms that you are serious about this type of work. Next he wants to know how you would react to a setback. Will you give up or will you persevere and keep looking? Finally he is probing for signs of self-doubt about your ability to handle the job.

Start by reiterating your interest and suitability for the role. Say that you have no doubt that you can do the job well. You are enthusiastic about working hard in the role. You feel that you would fit in well with the team. Say that you have been trying to convince the interviewer up to now of these facts. Ask if there is anything else that you need to reassure him about. If so, you have a great chance of reassuring him about any doubts he may still retain.

Only then should you explain what you would do if you were not offered the job. Say that you would carry out a post interview analysis to look at areas where you could have improved on your performance. You would correct any mistakes you made at interview. You would look at ways to overcome any shortcomings in your experience. You would then continue to look for similar work, as you believe that you are ideally suited for this type of job.

Have you received any other job offers?

It is acceptable to confirm other job offers. You will appear a more desirable prospect to the interviewer. You just need to say that would prefer to work with his company. Explain why you would rather work for them. Concentrate on why you are attracted to the company, rather than the job, if your other offer is in a similar role.

What would you be looking for in an employer?

Every company has its own unique culture. The interviewer is trying to discover if you would be comfortable working with theirs.

Keep this in mind when you prepare an answer to this question. Read the company's mission statement. Check the recruitment section of its website and sales brochures. They will stress things in which the company takes pride. Look out for phrases such as leading innovator, customer focused, or employee centred. This will help you construct your answer to this question.

If the company boasts about its training facilities, say that you are looking for an employer who invests in the training and development of its staff. Perhaps the company is proud of its employee relations. In this case just say that you value a company that communicates well and listens to the suggestions of its employees. If the company has an internal promotion policy, say that you like to work for a company that recognises and rewards hard work and commitment.

Do not say that you want a relaxed informal atmosphere. Do not say that you like to be allowed to get on with the job. Do not say that you do not like red tape. All of these answers would suggest difficulties with authority.

What sort of manager do you prefer to work for? Can you describe your ideal boss?

The interviewer wants to know if you will be comfortable working for your new boss.
He is also seeking an insight into your attitude to authority in general.

Be very careful how you answer this question. You do not know the management style of your prospective new boss. If you describe the wrong type of boss you may be rejected as incompatible.

Keep your answer as general as possible. If you have a lot of experience, say that you have worked for a lot of different bosses with different management styles. You managed to work effectively with all of them.

Do not talk about problems with previous bosses. Do not give the impression that you have any problems following orders or procedures. Do not say that you would prefer an easy going boss. This gives the impression that you are looking for an easy time.

Say that you prefer a boss who sets challenging targets. One who delegates tasks. One who expects the best from his people. One who offers constructive feedback. You like to keep your boss informed of your progress. You review your work with your boss at agreed intervals, to make sure that he is happy with the progress. You have learned a great deal from your previous bosses. You hope to continue to do so in the future.

You have remained in your previous job for a long time. Why do you want to move now?

The interviewer's main concern is that you have become stagnant. You are set in your ways and lack inspiration. You will struggle to adjust to a new working environment. You lack the breadth of experience of someone who moved about more.

You need to stress the variety in your old job. Give examples of:

- Additional responsibility.
- Variety of assignments.
- Participation in development projects.
- Covering for your boss.
- Interaction with other departments.
- Additional training and qualifications.
- How you advocated change and better ways of doing things.

You need to impress that every day was a new challenge. It was not just the same old job all the time. You grew and developed continuously in the role.

You can add that you enjoyed the challenging environment. You got on well with fellow employees. You wanted to remain loyal to the firm. You now wish to move on and broaden your experience by taking on new challenges.

Why have you changed jobs so often?

Changing jobs often suggests a lack of commitment to previous employers. There is a reluctance to hire job hoppers in case they leave after a short period for a better offer elsewhere.

Explain your reasons without saying anything negative about your previous employers. This will only reinforce the interviewer's concerns. Point out that you have worked hard while in each position and put the firm's interests first.

Give valid reasons for as many of the moves as possible. Perhaps you were made redundant. Maybe the company closed your department and you moved to remain in your chosen career path. Perhaps you took a job in one region, hoping for a transfer nearer home. When none became available you took an opportunity closer to home. Maybe the contract was short term, or the job was temporary. Perhaps the job was a stop gap until you found a position related to your chosen career path.

In the absence of any valid reasons say that you wished to broaden your experience. You wanted to do this early in your career. You believe that the broad experience you have gained will be an asset. You now wish to settle in this career path with their company.

Finish by explaining just how committed you are to the job and the firm.

How long do you think you would stay in this job if you got it?

The recruitment process for a permanent role is expensive. A lot of money, time and effort will go into drawing up the job specification, advertising the role, short listing, interviewing and final selection. The company needs to get the choice right. They need a return for their investment. They want to hire someone who will settle happily in the role. They want someone who will contribute for several years to come.

Simply answer that you would like to make a long term commitment to the firm. You want to develop your career with them. You are confident you would be successful in the job. You will work hard in the role, achieve results and prove your worth. You are sure that, given time, you could take on extra responsibilities. You could make a valid, worthwhile, contribution to the company for years to come.

Chapter 33. Questions that are negative or deliberately challenging

For most candidates negative questions are the most difficult type to answer. If you are asked a negative question, remain calm and objective. Remember that the interviewer is simply doing his job. He is pointing out where he feels that your experience and skills are not a perfect match to his requirements.

Alternatively the interviewer may be deliberately putting you under pressure to see how you cope. You may be required to cope with pressure and unexpected situations in the job. You may need to be able to think on your feet. Perhaps you will be expected to deal with awkward clients, or unhappy customers.

Negative or challenging questions give you an excellent opportunity to sell yourself. Many candidates struggle with negative questions. So if you can answer them well it will set you apart from the competition.

The secret to answering negative questions is to respond in a positive manner. Demonstrate emotional maturity by talking objectively and honestly about your experiences.

- Take your time and think rationally before you respond.
- Remain calm and composed.
- Do not take it personally.
- Detach yourself from all emotions.
- Do not get rattled.
- Do not argue with the interviewer.
- Do not appear defensive, evasive or confrontational.
- Be professional and stick to the issues.
- Give explanations and mitigating circumstances.
- If the issue occurred some time ago, point this out.
- Concentrate on what you learned from the experience.
- Show how you have matured and developed over time.
- Point out that you regularly review performance.

- Show that you work towards personal goals.
- Show that you welcome all criticism as an opportunity to develop.

Remember that all interview questions are asked for one of three reasons. You need to work out quickly which one is relevant to the question and answer it accordingly. The three things the interviewer wants to know are:

- Do you have the skills, experience and personal attributes to do the job?
- Will you work hard and contribute in terms of results?
- Will you settle in harmoniously with the existing team?

Even the tough or negative questions are geared to answering one of these fundamental issues. You need to be clear in your mind which issue is of concern. You can then tackle it head on in your response. You can reassure the interviewer that his doubts are unfounded.

You don't seem to have the experience we are looking for.

If you didn't have the minimum requirements, you would not be sitting in your seat listening to this question. The company would not have wasted time and money on inviting you to the interview.

If you are asked this question, then the company has probably short listed some older candidates with more experience for interview. Remember the company is not looking for the most qualified candidate. Many people are overqualified. The company is looking for the closest match to the specified job requirements. Focus your answer on showing how closely you match the job criteria.

Employers can no longer discriminate on the basis of age. So they will ask this question when they really think that you are too young for the role. Employers have specific concerns about younger candidates. It is not really the lack of skill and experience. Their big fear is that younger applicants will be less reliable, less committed to the firm and more likely to move on sooner.

In answering the question you need to highlight the additional personal skills you possess. You also need to stress your long term commitment to the job. Emphasise your desire to develop your experience and skills with the company.

Younger candidates have a number of distinct advantages. Work some of these into your reply. Younger candidates are perceived as being:

- Willing to learn.
- Easier to train.
- More adaptable and enthusiastic.
- More willing to work shift patterns or travel.
- More computer literate.
- Less likely to miss work due to ill health.
- Less likely to have acquired bad habits.
- Less likely to have become set in their ways.

You may be asked this question if you will be expected to supervise older employees. If you have experience of supervising older staff, then detail this.

Explain that performance is dependent on an individual's level of motivation, not the depth of their experience. Point out that you obviously have the minimum requirements. What really is important is attitude. You are willing to work hard, take on new challenges and meet targets. Finish by saying that you regularly review your behaviour and develop new ways of improving your performance.

You look to be too experienced for this job. Don't you feel you are overqualified for this position?

This is a very tricky one. The interviewer's main concern is that you will take this job as a stop gap. You will leave as soon as a better offer comes up. Can you take orders from a younger, perhaps less experienced, boss? How will you relate to younger, less qualified colleagues?

Point out that you would not have applied if you didn't think you were right for the job. After all, the best teams are made up from individuals with varying areas of expertise and different levels of experience.

List the specific advantages you can bring:

- You can make a worthwhile contribution immediately.
- The company does not need to spend any money to train and develop you.
- You are mature, reliable and professional.
- You are committed, enthusiastic and dependable.
- You have a track record of working well as a team player.
- You can bring an abundance of experience to the firm.
- You have encountered and overcome most problems in the past.
- You have learned to deal with all sorts of personalities.
- You can take on extra duties and responsibilities.
- You can help develop younger, less experienced colleagues.

Point out that you want to make a long term commitment to the company. You would like to contribute to their success and are sure that you could be a valued member of the team.

If you perform well at the interview you might even be asked to apply for a more senior role with the company.

How would you react if I said that you were not the best candidate we've spoken to today?

Remain calm and ask the interviewer to be more specific. Ask him where he thinks you do not match up to his requirements. Then focus on giving him additional examples of your experience and achievements in that area. Show how this could benefit the company. It may be that you are actually weaker in this area. In this case, introduce some transferable skills that will help contribute to your success.

Remind the interviewer that what is most important is self-motivation. Willingness to work hard, dedication and perseverance are the most important qualities to succeed in any role. You have these in abundance and are convinced that you can succeed and surpass any expectations he holds.

Say that you feel you would fit in well and could quickly contribute in many ways to the overall team success. The interviewer may still have some lingering doubts about your experience, which is one of the three main determinants in allocating the job. However you have left him in no doubt about the other two major deciding factors. These are your willingness to perform to the best of your ability in the job and the likelihood that you will integrate well with the existing team.

Why have you not achieved more in your last job?

You may be asked this question if you were employed in the same job for a long time.
The employer will be concerned that you lack ambition and initiative.

You need to remain calm and be assertive. Say that you have achieved quite a lot. Give specific examples of your achievements. Show how they have benefited your employer. Show how the experience you gained could assist in the new role.

You may have retained the same job title, but moved up through different salary bands. Explain how the role broadened and how you took on additional duties and responsibilities. Perhaps you supervised more people, your budget increased or you looked after more clients. Perhaps you were upgraded temporarily to fill in for your boss. Talk about any performance related salary increases.

If you have had to turn down the opportunity for promotion due to family or personal commitments then explain this. Perhaps you had to care for a relative or were unable to relocate due to family commitments. Reassure the interviewer that your personal circumstances have since changed. You can now devote your full attention to your career. You are really keen to further your career with their company.

You seem to have been out of work for some time? Why is this?

If there are any employment gaps on your CV then you need to be prepared to talk about them. If you have a valid reason such as personal ill health, looking after a sick relative or raising a family, then give it. Otherwise the best thing to say is that you did not want to take the first opportunity that came along. You wanted a job that fitted into your chosen career path. You have been waiting for an opportunity like this one.

Show that you were not completely idle during any gaps in your career. Give examples of any temporary, voluntary or part time work or study. Say that you undertook these to enhance your longer term prospects. You need to demonstrate that you used your time constructively. In the current economic climate many applicants undergo periods of unemployment.

Can you tell me about a time when you were passed over for promotion?

This is a difficult question to answer. If you have been turned down for promotion the worst thing you could do is complain about the person who got the job. Never state that this person did not deserve the promotion. Do not complain that you had to work for someone less experienced than yourself. The interviewer will assume that you over estimate your own abilities and that you are a difficult subordinate.

The ideal answer is to give an example of how you overcame a setback. You were initially turned down for a promotion, but later secured the job when it was re-advertised. You were initially disappointed, but were determined to succeed. You met with the company. You asked where they felt you did not meet the job requirements. You assured them that you would work on these areas. You congratulated the successful candidate and got on with the job. You paid extra attention to the areas needing improvement.

In the long run your perseverance and dedication won through. You got the job.

You don't seem to have the qualifications we are asking for

If you are obviously missing some specified requirement there is no point in arguing about the merits of the qualification. If the employer felt that the qualification was essential you would not have been invited to the interview. It therefore must be a desirable factor. Something that is likely to swing the decision someone else's way if the balance of all other factors ended up equal.

So what you need to do is show that you have compensating qualifications or, more likely, additional experience. The lack of this qualification has not in any way hampered your performance up to now. In fact it has made you work harder and achieve more. You believe that success is directly related to the right attitude and the level of commitment.

If you are currently studying for this qualification or similar award then point this out.

How would you feel about having to take instructions from a younger boss?

You are less likely to be asked this question since recent legislation has been introduced to cover discrimination on the basis of age. The implication is that you are too old and set in your ways.

The answer is that you are sure that the company promotes on merit alone. Age is just a number. People are promoted on performance, results and attitude. Regardless of who you report to, you assume that they got the position on merit.

The age of the person would have no effect on your relationship.

Chapter 34. Questions you should not be asked at interview

UK equal opportunity laws exist to protect employees. This includes all internal or external candidates applying for a job. There are a number of topics you should not be asked about at interview. This is because it is illegal to discriminate against employees on certain grounds. These characteristics are deemed to be irrelevant to their ability to carry out the job to the required standard.

If you are asked an illegal question it is up to yourself whether you answer or not. The manager conducting the interview may be inexperienced at the task and ignorant of the law. You may choose to answer the question. Alternatively you could ask the employer to explain how the question relates to the specified job requirements. You could also blatantly point out that the question is illegal and refuse to answer it. However, unfortunately, this would probably harm your prospects of getting a job offer.

You should not be asked the following types of questions:

- Questions on nationality or place of birth, including questions about race or ethnic origin.
- Questions about your religious denomination or beliefs.
- Questions relating to your gender.
- Questions about your age.
- Whether you are married, engaged, separated or divorced.
- How you intend to arrange for child care.
- Whether you intend to have children.
- What you would do if your children became ill.
- Membership of trade unions or political activities.
- Questions on sexual preferences.
- Questions about health or physical disabilities.
- Questions about lifestyle choices such as alcohol or drug consumption.

Chapter 35. Questions to ask the interviewer

Selection is a two way process

The interview is a two way process. The interviewer will try to establish if you are the right person for the job. He will ask questions to confirm that this is the right job for you. Likewise you should ask questions to help you determine if the job is the right choice for you. You should ask clarifying questions throughout the interview. You also need to reserve several questions to the end of the interview. Keep your questions open-ended.

Questions at the start of the interview

There are two questions you must ask right at the beginning of the interview. Ask these questions before you answer any of the interviewer's questions. Ask about the scope and responsibility of the role and the qualities of an ideal candidate. Just explain that you want to make the most of your limited time together. You want to ensure that you direct your answers towards his most pressing needs and greatest priorities.

The answer to both questions should confirm what you already know from your research. This will allow you to begin selling your skills and suitability.

The answer might be slightly different from what you anticipated. The interviewer might place greater emphasis on some aspect of the job, perhaps not specified in the advertisement. If the answer differs from what you expected you can adjust your approach to suit. You could avoid emphasising some point which the interviewer believes to be less relevant.

Questions during the interview

Ask questions throughout the interview. This allows you to show interest, build rapport and clarify points before giving your answers. The tactic also allows you to introduce additional supporting information. If the interviewer probes into any areas, ask him directly what his concerns are. Then reassure him by giving additional examples to promote your suitability.

Questions at the end of the interview

You should be given the opportunity to ask your own questions when the interview is coming to a close. If you are not offered this chance, just say that you would like to ask a few questions of your own. The questions you ask can make the difference between receiving a job offer and being rejected.

Why you need to ask questions

Your questions should demonstrate how seriously you are considering taking up the role. They should be directed towards gaining more information about the job and what it would be like to work for the employer. Use your questions to illustrate that:

- You have listened attentively during the interview.
- You are really interested in the job and the organisation.
- You will work hard if you get the job.
- You would like to contribute as part of the team.

The interview is coming to a close. This is your last chance to supply any additional supporting information. The interviewer may be unskilled at the task. He may have covered the essential criteria, but failed to ask you to provide any additional supporting information. You must include this information while asking your questions. For every answer you receive, include a very brief statement to show that you have the matching experience.

You must reserve a few intelligent questions to help impress the interviewer. Work out and write down your questions in advance. Bring them with you. It is easy to become flustered and forget what you were going to ask. If you have a list, there is no problem in referring to it. This shows that you have done your research in advance and thought about the issues.

Select some questions that remain unanswered from your list. Aim to ask about three or four questions. There will usually not be time to ask more. Not asking any questions implies that you are not interested in the job. This is one of the biggest mistakes you can make at interview. Your questions should differentiate you from the opposition. They should demonstrate that you have seriously considered the role.

Sample questions you could ask

- How has the vacancy arisen?
- How long did the last person hold the position?
- Has anyone previously failed in this position? Why?
- How does the job fit into the company's organisation structure?
- How many people will report to the successful candidate?
- What is the makeup and strengths of the current team?
- What qualities would the ideal candidate bring to this role?
- What are your major concerns about filling this position?
- What resources will you make available to get the job done?
- If the role is new, why is it being set up?
- What is the first problem that needs tackled by the job holder?
- What are the immediate priorities?
- What are the main challenges in the role?
- What needs to be achieved in the first year?
- How will my performance be measured?
- How does the company view the role?
- How will the role develop?
- How will the job holder interact with other departments?
- What are the criteria for promotion?
- What is the likely progression path from this role?
- What training is available for advancement in the role?
- Does the company have an internal promotion policy?
- What is a realistic time frame for advancement?
- Is there a formal appraisal system?
- Can the job holder study for professional qualifications?
- Are there any special projects that need additional volunteers?
- Do you have any concerns about my ability to do the job?

- What concerns do I need to cover, for you to see me as the leading candidate?
- If you had to sell this job to me, how would you do it?

Reasoning behind your questions

Base your questions on how you would perform in the role. Ask the interviewer to explain the most urgent problems that need to be tackled in the job. This gives an insight into the immediate supervisor's thinking. You can then give examples of how you have solved similar issues.

How long the last person worked in the role might indicate the promotion possibilities. Beware if the interviewer is reluctant to say why the vacancy arose. There may have been relationship problems in the role. If last incumbent did not stay long, the boss may be difficult to work with.

Directly ask if anyone failed in the role and ask for specific reasons. If this has occurred you get the immediate supervisors perspective. You learn what is important to him. You learn the pitfalls to avoid in the role. You get the opportunity to reassure him that you would not make the same mistakes. You can explain that your personal skills and attributes would prevent this from happening.

Ask what the ideal candidate would bring to the role. You will get the interviewer's concept of the ideal candidate. You can then focus on how you have exactly the qualities he needs.

Asking about his major concerns about filling the role goes about the issue from the opposite perspective. Now you can see what he wants to avoid in anyone he hires. When he specifies his main concerns, you can demonstrate how you do not possess any of these draw backs.

If you ask how your performance will be measured, you will get the interviewer's viewpoint on what is required to be successful in the role. You will again be able to match your skills and reassure him about any concerns.

Asking about the current make up of the existing team shows that you are genuinely interested. You should ask a question about the immediate priorities. This helps the interviewer to gain a mental picture of you in the role. Subconsciously the interviewer begins to move you from the possible to the probable short list.

You could ask about the current structure of the job and how it fits into the organisation. Alternatively you could ask about how you would interact with other departments or customers. This shows that you have considered the wider implications of the job.

Be careful how you ask about training. You do not want to convey doubt in your abilities. Do not ask about initial training in the job. You can ask about training to help your promotion possibilities.

Asking about promotion indicates a long term commitment to the firm. This reassures the interviewer about one of his biggest concerns. He is worried about investing a lot of time and money on recruitment, only to have the selected candidate leave after a few months.

Overcome any final objections

Ask the interviewer if he has any remaining concerns about your suitability for the role. Listen carefully to how he replies. If there are any lingering doubts you will not receive a job offer. So this is your last chance to convince him that you the right person for the job. If you ask why you should not be the leading contender, you are placing yourself where you want the interviewer to perceive your worth.

Make them sell you the job

Finish by asking the interviewer to sell you the job. This shows that you are genuinely interested and seriously considering accepting the role. By making the interviewer sell you the job you are encouraging him to subconsciously make you an offer to join the company. You will be perceived as being more valuable to him. Thank the interviewer for doing a great job in selling the role. Tell him you are excited about the role and would love to accept an offer.

Weaker questions

Do not ask questions on information that you could easily have unearthed as part of your research into the company.

You can ask general questions about the company or the industry. However they do not help the interviewer to visualise you in the role.

Do not challenge any points the interviewer has made during the interview. Do not ask leading questions. This indicates you have already made your mind up on the answer.

Do not ask questions outside the interviewer's remit. He will feel uncomfortable if he is unable to answer. He will also fail to see the relevance. Stick to the job and your performance in it. Do not ask questions that require the interviewer to divulge confidential information.

Do not ask questions beginning with the question 'why'. Such questions can be viewed as confrontational.

What if the interviewer has answered my questions already?

This situation should not occur. You should be able to ask several questions from the above list that have not been covered during the body of the interview. You should be able to ask questions about how you would perform in the role. You can ask about how your performance would be measured. You could ask questions about the interviewer's concerns about your suitability. If there are any other issues that will influence your decision to take the job you should ask before you leave.

Do not ask self-interest questions

Your questions need to be focused on what you can bring to the job. Do not ask questions about what the company can do for you. Do not ask about:

- Salary or other negotiable terms and conditions.
- Company benefits.
- Holiday entitlements.
- Length of working week.
- Flexible working hours.
- Job sharing.
- Health insurance.
- Having to relocate.
- Whether you need to work weekends or overtime.
- Whether you would get your own office.
- How you performed in the interview.
- The number or nature of other candidates.
- Trade union membership.
- Company social clubs or sports facilities.

Questions on salary, terms and conditions can be resolved if you receive a job offer.

The interviewer will not be able to tell you if you have been successful at this stage. He needs to complete his scoring sheet, add up your marks and consult with colleagues after you have left. There will probably be other candidates to interview first. Other factors such as references, medical and test scores need to be taken into account before any final decision.

Chapter 36. Post interview analysis

Review your performance

Practice makes perfect. The interview is a performance. You need to rehearse thoroughly, like any good actor does, before every interview. Also, just like an actor can improve with every recital, so will your performance improve with every interview you attend. However, the best actors study their lines, rehearse thoroughly and analyse their performance in minute detail. Every nuance, every gesture, every pause, every intonation is honed and polished until the actor feels he cannot improve on the performance.

Just like the actor, you should treat every interview as a learning process. You will learn more efficiently if you analyse your performance each time. You will discover ways in which you can improve on your performance next time.

However the actor is given more help analysing his performance than you are able to take benefit from. He will usually have a mentor or friend in the audience. He will have feedback from the other participants, the director and the critics. He can analyse the reaction from the crowd. The performance may have been filmed or the sound recorded. At the interview itself you only have the reaction of the interviewers to go on. If you are later rejected for the position, you will usually only be told that you were not the best fit.

Act immediately

It is therefore crucial that you carry out a prompt and thorough post interview analysis. Do this as soon as possible after leaving the interview premises. Every minute you delay will reduce your ability to recall what transpired in detail.

You can use the preparation notes you had for interview. This will contain the questions you anticipated being asked and your prepared answers. Tick off the questions they asked. Underline the sections you remembered to answer. Jot down any follow up questions they had for these questions and how you responded. Make a note of any questions they asked that you did not anticipate. Note how you responded. Get as much detail down on paper as quickly as possible.

Questions to consider

Consider the following and make further notes where appropriate:

- Did you arrive on time?
- Was your appearance right for the job?
- Did you overlook anything in your research?
- Did the job differ from what you anticipated? Did you find out about this early enough in
the interview? Why did you form the wrong impression from the job advertisement? How will you avoid this happening again?
- Should you have found out more about the job in advance?
- Did you make a good initial impression?
- Did you settle down quickly?
- Did you behave in a confident manner throughout?
- Did interview nerves hamper your performance?
- Did you show enough enthusiasm for the job?
- Did you smile and make enough eye contact?
- Did you encounter problems building rapport with the interviewer? Why?
Was the interviewer skilled at his job? Did you have to guide him with your answers? How can you do this better in future?
- Did the interviewer leave out any of your anticipated questions? Why was this not important to him?
- Did you struggle with any difficult questions? Were there questions you just could not answer? Why were the questions asked? How can you prepare suitable answers for future interviews?
- Did you forget to include any information? Can you work this into one of your answers to the common interview questions? Should you include this information in your CV?

- Did the interview focus on any skills that you were lacking? Can you undergo any training to acquire these skills?
- Was the interviewer concerned about any issues? Was he unhappy with any of your answers? Were you able to overcome his doubts? How can you improve on your answers?
- Do you need to alter your CV? Can you steer the conversation away from these issues in future?
- Did you reveal any weaknesses you wished to conceal? How can you avoid this happening next time?
- Did you focus enough on the vacancy? Were you able to demonstrate your suitability for the role? Did you match your skills to the job requirements? Could you have used better examples?
- Did you ask the right questions? How did the interviewer react to your questions? Could you improve on your questions?
- Did you miss an opening? Should you have been listening better? How well did you present your case? Can you improve on this in future?

Salvaging the situation

No one is perfect. Nobody gives the perfect performance. There will be areas in which you could have done better. The good news is that you still have a chance to salvage the situation. You can still strengthen your case. You still have time to act. The interview process will probably take a few more days. It then usually takes a few days to come to a decision. The interviewers need this time to collate all the relevant information and compare the performance of the candidates. You may be in the final reckoning. There may be little to choose between yourself and another favoured candidate. You might just tip the balance in your favour by sending a follow up letter based on your post interview analysis.

The follow up letter

The follow up letter strengthens your case because:

- You can include information you forgot at interview.
- You can redress where you came across as weak at interview.
- It demonstrates that you are committed.

- It shows a degree of courtesy.
- It brings your application to the fore front.

Address the letter to the interviewers, thanking them and reaffirming your interest in the job.

Send the letter by first class mail as soon as possible. It must arrive before the final selection decision has been made. You could follow up by email, but letters are best.

If you forgot some critical point at the interview give brief details in the follow up letter.

The follow up letter should be kept to one page and convey that you:

- Wish to thank them for their time.
- Enjoyed meeting with the interviewers.
- Were delighted to learn more about the firm and the job.
- Are very keen on the job.
- Possess the skills and experience to do the job.
- Would be very committed to the role.
- Would fit in well with the existing team and culture.
- Have summarised any additional relevant points not covered at interview.
- Would like to add information that you omitted during the interview.
- Would be delighted to receive a job offer or invite to follow up interview.

Contacting the firm

You will have been promised a response on the outcome of the interview within a given time frame. It is not unusual for companies to take longer than promised.
If this happens just allow a few extra days. Then ring the personnel office. Ask when you are likely to receive any update. You should give your name, the job title, the date of the interview and the interviewer's name.

Coping with rejection

Do not be disheartened if you are rejected for the job. Do not take it personally. Do not let it affect your self-worth. Rejection is an integral part of the process. Keep things in perspective. Most people are unsuccessful at their first interview. They usually need to attend several interviews before securing an offer. If you apply the lessons from this book you will improve your chances of securing an offer. However it is essential to apply for jobs at the level of your experience, for which you are qualified.

If you are rejected for a job you need to understand the reason. Were you under qualified or overqualified in any way? Were your competencies not considered a close enough match to the job requirements? You could ring up the personnel department and politely ask for advice on your performance. However companies are very reluctant to divulge any information of this nature. They usually say that you were simply not the best fit. Unfortunately this vague answer sheds little light on the situation.

Persevere

The very best candidates get turned down on occasions. A lot of applicants will have been chasing a limited number of places. That is the nature of the process. For every successful candidate there can be hundreds who failed to get the offer. Never get discouraged or lose heart. We all face setbacks.

The interview is like an audition for an actor. You have to apply for many roles before landing an offer. Every interview is a learning process and no interview is a waste of time. We can all improve with practice. Every rejection takes you one step closer to being accepted. If you are better prepared for the next interview, you will have a better chance of getting the offer.

Never blame an interviewer for your failure to get the job. Even if he was inexperienced and unprofessional, you should have overcome this and introduced the pertinent facts. Concentrate on what you have learned from the experience. Apply this knowledge at the next interview.

Losing out to an internal candidate

Perhaps the job was offered to an internal candidate. You might be able to find this out from someone you know who works for the firm. Companies regularly opt for an internal candidate. This person has more knowledge of the job, the firm and the operating procedures. Internal candidates require little or no induction. They have a proven track record. They represent a safe bet, compared with the risks and uncertainties of taking on an external candidate.

You can take advantage of this fact. Many companies have an internal promotion policy. They will always seek to fill a vacancy from current employees before searching elsewhere. You can apply for a lower job with the company just to get your foot in the door. You can then access the many internal vacancies that are not advertised outside the company.

Letter of reply to rejection

Always write a letter of reply to your rejection letter. This is probably the last thing you feel like doing when you get a rejection letter. However it is a good tactic for two reasons. Firstly the successful applicant may not settle in the role and leave within a few months. If this situation arises, the company will first review the previously short listed candidates. Your professionalism in reconfirming your interest might secure a further interview.

Secondly you can ask about other vacancies that might come up. Just acknowledge that, although you were unsuccessful this time, you were very impressed with the company. You would be very interested if any similar vacancies were to arise. Ask for your application to be kept on file for this eventuality.

Seeking professional help

If you have been rejected a number of times, consider the following action to improve your prospects:

- Consult with your local careers advisor.
- Attend mock interviews.
- Join a job search club.
- Obtain extra qualifications from part time study.
- Consider part time, temporary or voluntary positions.

Chapter 37. Negotiating the job offer

Never negotiate early

Never negotiate salary during a job interview. The selection process is still ongoing. There will still probably be outstanding candidates to interview. The company will not have scored your performance, or be ready to make a job offer. You could price yourself out of the job. You will also be negotiating from a position of weakness, since the company still has a choice of candidates. You may not even be talking to the person who has the authority to agree wage rates.

If the interviewer asks you about salary requirements, just say that you will be happy to discuss this if you receive a confirmed job offer. Ask if you are being offered the job. If not, do not be drawn into any negotiations. Stall the interviewer. You may be asked to give your current salary. Just answer that it would not be a direct comparison, because of all the associated terms and conditions. Say that you would prefer to discuss the job requirements in detail.

Wait until the company makes a job offer

Negotiations should only begin after you receive a job offer. At this stage the company will have only one or two reserve candidates. The workload caused by the vacant position will be building. Your potential future boss will be anxious to close the deal and get on with other things. The salary will be coming out of his budget. He will have authority to set the agreed rate.

At this stage everyone will appreciate that you are the best option. People expect to pay more for the best. You will not know it, but you could be the only suitable candidate. This puts you in a much stronger situation. In any case, the company will not want to lose you and settle for second best. Worse still, they do not want to repeat a costly recruitment exercise. The likely outcome would be an alternative candidate of the same standard. There is no guarantee that this person would accept a lower salary than you. The company are more inclined to increase your offer by ten or fifteen percent than to face the risky and costly alternatives.

The conditional offer

You may receive a conditional offer of employment. Look out for such a clause on any written offer. The job offer will be stated as being conditional on certain requirements being fulfilled. The usual condition is receipt of satisfactory references. You may be asked to furnish evidence of qualifications or a work permit. The offer may depend on you passing a medical examination.

Treat any conditional offers with extreme caution. Do not give in your notice to your current employer, or reject other offers of employment. Always secure a firm, negotiated and agreed written offer before terminating any other arrangements.

The telephone offer

You may receive a phone call from personnel to inform you that the company is willing to offer you the job. They might explain that they are ready to send you a written offer and then tell you the salary they expect to pay. They just want you to confirm the amount so that they can include it in the written offer.

This tactic is aimed at catching you off guard. In your elation at getting the offer they hope to get you to concede to a lower salary than you would otherwise accept.

Thank the company for the offer. Ask them to send you a draft of the main terms and conditions in writing. Tell them that they can leave the salary details blank at this stage. Once you have considered the other terms and conditions you will be quite happy to meet with them and discuss the salary details. If they insist on putting a salary figure on the draft offer then tell them that you consider it to be negotiable. Arrange a meeting to discuss it. Make sure you have at least one day to go over the offer details.

The face to face offer

Sometimes if you are the last candidate to be seem at a final selection interview you may receive an offer on the spot. You might be told that the company would like to make you an offer. You might then be asked to let them know what salary you were considering. Be ready for this eventuality. Always do your salary and negotiating research in advance.

The written offer

Sometimes the job offer, salary details and main terms and conditions will arrive in writing by post. Ring the company up and arrange a meeting to discuss the detailed terms. You then can negotiate an improved deal.

The written offer should contain the following information:

- Details of both parties to the agreement.
- Job location and department.
- Job title.
- Job description and main responsibilities.
- Starting date.
- Relocation allowances.
- Induction details.
- Probation period.
- Hours of work.
- Holiday entitlement.
- Total pay package, including basic pay, overtime rate, bonuses, shift allowances, commissions, etc. Payment method and frequency should be given.
- Sick pay and benefits.
- Pension details.
- Medical or dental cover.
- Company car, travel allowances, etc.
- Employee discount schemes.
- Future salary potential.
- Request for you to confirm your acceptance of the offer.
- Notice of employment details.

- Disciplinary and grievance procedures.

Overcome the fear of negotiations

Most people are reluctant to ask for an improved job offer. Their main concerns are:

- They will look ungrateful for the job offer.
- They will get off to a bad start with their new boss and employer.
- They will appear demanding and troublesome.
- It will look as if they are only interested in themselves and not the team.
- Negotiating now will hamper future job increases and promotions.

You should not be anxious about asking for more. Budgets are flexible. All employers have some scope to negotiate. Employers expect you to fight your corner. By seeking a better deal, you will improve your perceived worth and status within the firm.

All future pay raises and rates are based on your starting salary. If you don't get the correct rate to begin with, it will remain wrong as long as you stay with this employer.

Be prepared to negotiate the job offer

Never, ever, accept the opening offer. Even if the offer looks good, you should negotiate it. It represents the minimum that the employer would like to pay. It is less than the figure that they expect they will have to pay. It will be less than they are paying other employees in similar jobs. It will be lower than the budgeted figure for the position.

Employers expect that they will have to increase opening offers. This is why they offer less than the budget figure. They also know that about one quarter of employees are willing to accept opening offers. They are banking on you being one of them. Do not undersell yourself. Get what you are worth. Negotiate. Only you can get them to move on the offer.

Never turn down an offer immediately

Never turn down a job offer immediately because it is less than you expected or wanted. Always negotiate first. If employers have made you an offer, then they consider you the best person for the job. They will almost always be prepared to move on any opening offer. Ring up the employer and ask for a meeting to discuss the offer. Then prepare your case, based on what you need from the deal.

If you have two offers, do not simply opt for the higher offer. You should consider both offers as being negotiable. Meet with both employers and bid them up. Bid one against the other if needs be.

Compare the total package with your current pay and conditions.

Before you decide on the job offer you need to look at a number of factors. Do you have all the details? Consider the total remuneration package including:

- Basic salary.
- Scheduled overtime.
- Shift premium.
- Bonus, commission, or incentive schemes.
- Basic contracted hours per week.
- Medical or dental insurance.
- Sick pay.
- Life assurance.
- Pension benefits.
- Company car or driving allowances.
- Subsidised travel.
- Paid tuition fees or training allowances.
- Holiday entitlement.
- Profit sharing.
- Crèche facilities or childcare allowance.
- Staff, product or service discounts.
- Recognition schemes.

- Other employee benefits.

Compare the total package you are being offered to your current earnings. The offer should exceed your current package. If the job offer is for a similar job you should aim for a ten per cent rise in total earnings. Work out your total current earnings package in advance of any meeting. Decide on your target salary package and the minimum you are prepared to accept. There are tax advantages in receiving certain benefits rather than a higher basic salary. However pension and life assurance are usually linked to basic salary. Future pay rises will also be linked to basic salary. Therefore you need basic salary to be as high as possible on entry to the firm.

Do not get caught out by the timing of the move. Your current employer may not have made an annual pay rise settlement just yet. Your new employer may have already settled theirs. Compare the new employer's offer with what you would have earned if you stayed in your existing job and took the pay rise.

Rules of the negotiating game

The main rule of negotiating is that anything goes. Expect to be confronted with negativity, hesitancy and resistance. It is the nature of the game. Recognise that the employer's behaviour is simply a role play. It is carried out for a specific purpose. Saving money.

Do not expect the company to play fair. Do not expect to be treated with kid gloves. This will be a no holds barred fight. Most companies will offer as little as possible. They will say that they have a limited budget. They will say that you have got your research wrong. You are over pricing yourself. They cannot afford your demands. They will hint at other candidates being willing to take such a generous offer. They will say that they cannot pay you more than their existing employees. They will try to undermine your credibility. They will try to wear you down.

They will try to put you under pressure. They will put a time limit on the offer. They will threaten to withdraw the offer. They will try all of these tactics and more to force you into accepting an offer on their terms. They will do anything and everything to sign you up, as soon as possible, for as little as they can get away with.

As far as job offers go, you do not get what you deserve. You get what you are prepared to negotiate. This may seem unfair to you. However the company has a business to run. To do this they must maximise profits. One way of doing this is to minimise total costs, which includes labour costs.

The negotiating process

You seldom get anything in this life without asking for it. This is particularly true when considering job offers. If you want a better package you need to be prepared to ask for it. No one else is going to do it for you. The best time to negotiate any salary is after you receive a job offer, but before you accept it.

Salary negotiations always involve a conflict of interests that no one wants to lose. They employee wants to secure as good a deal as possible. He believes he should get the going rate for his efforts. The company wishes to pay out as little as possible. Any costs are coming straight off the bottom line and will affect profitability. These costs will be ongoing, as it is not likely that wages will ever go down. There is an atmosphere of uncertainty. Neither side really knows what the other side is prepared to settle for. No one knows the outcome from the start.

Negotiations follow a familiar pattern. The company will make an opening offer. This will be less than they are willing to concede. You then ask for more than you hope to get. The haggling begins and eventually you meet somewhere in the middle. This is known as a win-win situation. Both parties are happy to walk away with something from the deal.

Your negotiating strategy

Do not try to negotiate every item in the pay and conditions package. The employer will assume that you are unreasonable and they will not be able to deal with you. Your first and main aim is to increase the basic salary, as several other benefits are linked to salary. You should then select about two other benefits that you want improved. Examples might be individual bonuses and severance terms. Consider the following points:

- You will never be in a stronger position.
- Carry out market research on salary rates in advance.
- Finalise the salary negotiations before negotiating other terms.
- Know your ideal goal, your likely target and your bottom line.
- Do not be limited by your previous salary. Do not disclose your previous salary. It will set a limit on your perceived worth.
- Ask for more than you want. They will be bidding you downwards.
- Do not be specific on your demands. Quote a range if needs be.
- Let them do the talking. Let them think that they are in the driving seat. The less you say the better. If you do the talking, they will simply pick holes in your argument. It also gives you time to read their signals and body language. Try to understand what they are implying, as well as what they are actually saying.
- Pension and bonuses are often linked to basic salary. This is another reason to negotiate increased salary first.
- Future employers will evaluate your worth on your basic salary history.
- You have more control over achieving individual bonuses, rather than group bonuses.
- Emphasising pay rates elsewhere will get you nowhere.
- Pleading your case in terms of cost of living will be futile.
- Know your worth. Stick to the benefits you can bring in terms of added value and efficiency savings.
- A unique skill set will enhance your position.
- The longer the job has remained unfilled, the stronger your position.
- Pointing out that your current pay and conditions are higher is valid. No one will expect you to move for less reward.
- If you are changing career, you are in a weaker position.

- If you are negotiating through a third party, such as a recruiter, you have less control over the process. The recruiter might be receiving a retainer from the company. Do not assume that they are acting in your interest.
- Do not accept a fancy title in lieu of the proper pay rate.
- Do not listen to future promises of growth, pay rises or promotion.
- As a last resort, if they won't increase the offer, try to get the job upgraded by agreeing to take on extra responsibilities. You may be solving another problem they have. The employer will feel that he is getting value for his money.
- Be firm. Ask for what you want, but don't issue demands and ultimatums. Remain professional and courteous at all stages. If you lock them into a position, they may withdraw the offer.
- Remain professional. Don't take things personally. Try to make the conversation light hearted. Smile and be friendly. Break the ice when you can. Try to avoid confrontation. This only makes people become entrenched.
- Know which terms and conditions that they are more likely to move on. Examples include relocation expenses, individual bonuses, severance pay, value of company car, expense accounts, and employee discount rates.
- You will be able to negotiate more if you are willing and able to walk away from the deal.
- If you know someone working for the company try to get additional information from them. They are unlikely to discuss their own salary. However they may, for example, give an indication of the prospects for advancement and the frequency that collective bonuses pay out.
- Listen carefully to what the employer is saying. They will give reasons for their objections. These will not apply to all the terms and conditions. Just because they cannot move on one aspect, does not mean that they are hampered in a similar manner elsewhere.
- Be prepared to make concessions, but not early in the process. Pick something that is less important to you. If you hint that you are prepared to make a concession the employer will feel obliged to reciprocate. You will be able to trade concessions. You may get something you want.

- Never come to an agreement without first asking for a day to consider the improved offer. Ask them to put it in writing. Make sure that they include everything that you have agreed upon.

The Company's viewpoint

- You are their first choice candidate. They will be prepared to pay a little more.
- They will offer as little as they can get away with.
- Their initial offer will be less than they have budgeted for the role.
- Their opening offer is almost always less than they are prepared to pay.
- They will expect to have to move on the initial offer, if you are not afraid to ask.
- They know that 25% of people are afraid to negotiate and accept initial offers. They are hoping you fall into this category.
- The strength of your position depends on the number and quality of reserve candidates they have.
- They prefer to settle as soon as possible. They do not want to lose you after protracted negotiations. Their reserve candidates may have secured offers from elsewhere.
- They want the position filled, as the workload will be building.
- The last thing they want is to have to re-advertise, with all the associated cost and disruption.
- They will usually be prepared to match comparable existing competitor rates within their geographical area.
- Pay rates vary with economic conditions. They are subject to the supply and demand of qualified applicants.
- The may be constrained by existing pay structures and salary bands.
- They do not want to rock the boat with existing employees.
- If there is no other similar role in the organisation, they do not need to conform to any existing pay rates.
- They have more lee-way for senior positions.
- You are an unknown and unproven quantity. There is an element of risk.

- A lot of the associated terms and agreements such as pension, life assurance, travel allowance and sick pay are collective agreements. They cannot make individual exceptions.
- They are more able to be flexible on one off costs, such as relocation expenses or severance pay. There will also be scope to negotiate bonus and commission rates.
- Smaller firms can often move more easily on salary rates.
- They may expect to pay new starts less and let them earn their salary increments by results.

Carry out preparation in advance

Many job advertisements give some indication of the likely salary. Some just indicate that the salary is negotiable. Most firms have a salary pay scale or salary band for a particular job. The more experience you have, or gain, the further up the band you can progress. As part of your research for the vacancy, you need to establish the likely salary range. Your aim is to be paid somewhere approaching the upper end of the salary band.

- Work out in advance the total value of your current package including benefits.
- You want the offer to exceed your current total package by 10% to 15% for the same job level. You need significantly more if you are applying for a promotion.
- Research on-line and get the average pay rates for the job. Work out the maximum you are likely to get. You should aim towards this ideal figure. Also know your bottom line, in terms of the minimum you are prepared to accept. Your target, or what you hope to get, is somewhere in between the two figures. This is the realistic figure that you should be able to achieve.
- Work out in advance where you can add value to the firm and pitch your sale accordingly.

Do not name your price

The critical thing about the negotiation process is not to name your price. Insist upon the employer makes the opening offer. Whoever makes the opening offer will be negotiating from a position of weakness. Continually knock the ball back into their court. Insist that they make the opening offer. It is their budget. They are buying. They want you. They need to make you an offer which attracts you. You are willing to listen to what they have to offer.

Initial offers define one limit of the negotiating zone. Once the employer makes the initial offer then this becomes the lower limit. This is your safety net. They cannot reduce this offer. You can negotiate upwards on this lower limit, by following the advice in this chapter. You immediately have the impetus. You have something to aim at. You have the upper hand. You are in control.

If you were foolish enough to make the opening demand, this would immediately become the upper limit. You will have declared your hand. You have nowhere to go but downwards. You have no idea of how low this will be. You have no safety net. You have no idea what the company's offer will be. You have handed the employer the initiative and control over the process. They will now offer much less than they are willing to pay. The figure will be considerably lower than you have demanded. You are more likely to feel negative and demeaned. You have an uphill battle to get anywhere near what you want. You will find it more difficult to listen and concentrate. You may become anxious.

The opening bid

- You will usually be outnumbered at the meeting. Do not let this intimidate you.
- Never, ever, make the opening bid. Whoever makes the opening bid is negotiating from a position of weakness.
- Never accept the company's opening offer. Just remain silent for as long as possible and look disappointed. At least 30 seconds.
- Never concede anything at the opening stage. If you do, your case will collapse.

The bargaining process

- Keep calm and do not display emotions. A low initial offer is not an insult or a measure of your personal worth. The company is just trying to save expenses. You would do the same if the roles were reversed. They expect to have to move on an initial offer.

- Bid them upwards. Say that you were anticipating a better offer. Do not specify your requirements. Throw the ball back into their court.

- Point out that you both know that you are the best candidate for the job.

- Express surprise at such a poor offer, after the firm has spent so much time and effort on an expensive recruitment exercise.

- Indicate that you are aware of the going market rate.

- Hint at your reluctance to take a better offer from elsewhere. You really don't want to work for the opposition. This will make them want to conclude the negotiations as soon as possible, rather than risk losing your services.

- If you are failing to make progress you can point out that your current package is higher.

- However this will set an upper limit on what you are likely to get.

- Be patient. Do not appear anxious to secure a deal. They are the ones with the vacancy that needs filling. Point out that you can only accept the job on the right terms.

- Point out that the savings you can bring to the firm far outweigh any salary costs.

- If you are getting nowhere on salary, then negotiate on the other terms.

- Do not let the company put a time pressure on you to sign any deal. They may say that they need to wind up to attend other meetings. Just tell them that you will be happy to meet later and conclude the negotiations.

Close the deal

- Once you have got what you want on your main terms you should concede a minor point to show flexibility. This allows for a win-win situation. Be prepared to move from your opening position. This way your future employer can feel that they have not lost out and have retained credibility.

- Never, ever, accept an offer to review your salary once you begin the job. Verbal offers are not worth the paper they are not written on! You can be guaranteed that the company's recollection of any promises diminish exponentially with time.

Failure to agree

Be prepared to walk away if they cannot meet your minimum requirements.

Negotiating tactics

Employers pay as little as they can get away with. Your aim is to get as much as possible. You can only obtain this by concentrating on what you can contribute to the company. They need to appreciate your worth in terms of any savings or improvements you can make. Hiring you needs to be a net benefit. They must see you as an asset that is worth investing in.

If you do not ask for the correct rate you will not be offered it. The company will have a salary band for the job. Place yourself towards the upper part of the scale. Your exact location will depend on your experience. So be realistic, but ask for more that you expect to receive. They will expect you to reduce your initial demands. If you have a lot of experience and qualifications you should be near the upper limit. Be prepared to justify your positioning.

If the employer's opening offer is too low, the best initial tactic is to say nothing. Remain silent for as long as possible. They might capitulate and improve the offer without you needing to argue your case. However they might be prepared to wait you out. If they do so, then just say that you feel that the job responsibilities and accountabilities warrant a better offer. You expect that the savings you can bring will far outweigh the cost of your salary. You are simply looking to receive the fair market value.

If you cannot get them to budge on basic salary then ask if they can improve on any other benefits. You might be able to get some productivity, sales or efficiency bonuses included in the package. Point out that this will be a self-financing exercise. It will only need to be paid out if you hit the targets and generate the additional revenue for the company.

Find out if salary review is based on performance appraisal. Ask if a recognised system is used. This gives you an opportunity to earn more than just cost of living rises in the future.

Ask about the type of pension on offer. Find out the contributions you would be expected to pay. Are payments index linked to inflation? Get advice on the pension before signing any contract.

Ask about the previous performance of collective bonus schemes. What are you really likely to earn from such schemes?

Don't get fobbed of with excuses or delaying tactics. Never, ever, accept a verbal promise of a future review after a period of service. This is totally worthless. The very least you can accept is a written agreement, signed by both parties, that your salary will increase to a specified amount after an agreed period. This must not be linked to satisfactory completion of a probation period. The company can easily rescind on the agreement based on their definition of 'satisfactory'.

Remember that you will be in a much weaker position six months down the line if they renege on promises. You will have difficulty trying to move on from a company if you have only stayed with them for a short period of time. Prospective employers will suspect that there were issues with your performance or that you had relationship problems with your boss.

Negotiation pitfalls to avoid.

- Naming your salary requirements before receiving an offer.
- Not equating total packages in making comparisons.
- Not taking into account financial implications of the timing of the move.
- Lack of research in advance.
- Settling for the initial offer.

- Turning down an offer immediately, instead of negotiating a better deal.
- Producing a list of demands.
- Making the opening bid.
- Talking too much.
- Aiming too low. Not asking for more than you want.
- Revealing your bottom line early in negotiations.
- Focusing on your requirements rather than on what you can contribute.
- Not being assertive enough.
- Becoming emotionally involved.
- Being aggressive or adversarial.
- Issuing ultimatums or drawing a line in the sand.
- Accepting future reviews, rather than immediate salary increases.
- Accepting bonuses that seldom pay out.
- Appearing anxious to settle.

If you make the mistake of making the opening bid you could under price yourself. The employer will probably accept immediately. This is a sure sign that they have got you for less than they budgeted. It is too late to ask for a higher basic salary. You should immediately request that you now negotiate the total package. Then ask for more in terms of bonuses and ancillary benefits.

Non salary items that you can negotiate.

- Company car - or better specification car.
- Laptop and mobile phone.
- Working from home.
- Home phone and internet payments.
- Increased employer contributions to your pension.
- Sponsored training for qualifications.
- Paid professional fees.
- Stock options.
- Profit sharing.
- Higher commission rate on bonuses.
- Medical or life insurance.
- Better employee discount rate or spend limits.

- Membership of clubs or associations.
- Discounts to events.
- Additional holidays.
- Flexible working arrangements.

Considering the offer.

Terms and conditions are not the only factor that you need to take into account when considering a job offer. Before accepting any offer of employment you need to consider the following:

- Have you considered all the implications of accepting the job?
- Do you need anything clarified before accepting the offer?
- Is the company the right choice?
- Can you handle the job?
- Will the work be challenging enough?
- Does the company have medium term stability and security?
- Do you feel comfortable with your prospective new boss?
- Will you be happy in the new environment?
- Will you find the work enjoyable?
- Will the job make the most of your talents, abilities and experience?
- Can you improve your skills in this role?
- Will you be given autonomy in the role?
- Will you have sufficient responsibility?
- Does the company provide training?
- Will you find the job interesting?
- How is the work life balance?
- Are there sufficient opportunities for internal promotion?
- How much of your time will the job, the commute and associated travel take up?
- What are the chances of promotion from this role?

Write a list of pros and cons for accepting the job offer. Compare the offer to your current position, or any offer you have from elsewhere. Remember no amount of salary can make up for choosing a job in which you are unhappy.

Do not let yourself be rushed into making a rash decision. Ask for two days to consider the offer. It is in the employer's interest that they select someone who fully considered the offer and will be happy in the job.

How does the offer compare with any other jobs to which you are applying? If you are waiting on a decision from another employer, stall the company by asking for more time to consider.

Accepting the written offer

Never accept a job offer until you have the complete offer in writing. If you negotiate a verbal offer, ask the employer to put the total offer, including benefits, in writing. Double check the details before signing any agreement. Always ask for time to consider the offer.

If the offer is less than your current package, you would need to have a good reason for accepting it. Other factors might influence your decision. The job may involve flexitime, job-sharing or working from home. There may be better prospects of promotion.

Check the written offer carefully. Make sure it reflects exactly what was agreed verbally. If you are not happy with any aspect, ring up and discuss the issue and your concerns. It may simply be a misprint.

The job offer will often refer to other policy or benefits documents. These are usually contained in the employee handbook. If this has not been provided, ring up and ask for a copy. Remember that there is usually a clause included in employee handbooks that terms and conditions are subject to change at any time.

If you are happy with the offer send a brief letter of acceptance to the firm. Address it to the person who made the offer and copy the human resources department. Thank them for the offer. Reiterate the agreed salary and main benefits. Refer to their written offer. Confirm your start date. Say that you are looking forward to starting the job. Keep a copy of this letter. Having formally accepted the offer in writing, it is very difficult for the company to withdraw it.

The contract of employment

Sometimes the firm will send you a contract of employment to sign in advance of your starting date. Sign and return this with your letter of offer. Some firms prefer to get you to sign the contract at induction. This allows them to explain all the detailed terms and conditions of employment. They can answer any questions you have. This protects them better if they later have to discipline you for any breaches. They can prove that they covered all the details at induction.

Rejecting the offer

You may not be able to negotiate an offer meeting your minimum requirements. If you are unhappy with the offer you should write a letter politely declining it. Briefly point out your reasons and say that you must reluctantly turn down the offer. Perhaps the total package is less than you are currently receiving. Maybe you got a better offer elsewhere. Your current employer might have given you an improved offer to retain your services.

It is important to remain polite and professional. Thank the company for the offer and the opportunity of meeting them. You never know, you may get an improved offer.

Remember that accepting an offer with which you are unhappy could adversely affect your future well being. You may resent the employer for undervaluing your worth. Your performance may be affected. This will harm your career prospects.

Dealing with multiple job offers

Many applicants apply to several jobs simultaneously. Having made the decision to leave their existing employer, they send out multiple applications. Graduates and school leavers, seeking their first full time job, often apply to multiple vacancies.

If you are a particularly strong candidate, you may receive more than one job offer.

Show common courtesy and write to politely decline any job offers that you do not intend to take up. Thank each of the companies involved and give your reason for turning down the offer. You may wish to apply to this firm at some stage in your future career. There is no point destroying the positive impression you have established with them.

Chapter 38. Leaving your existing employer

Giving your notice

Adapt a professional approach when resigning from your current employer. You may well require a reference from this employer in the future. You must:

- Tell your boss first, face to face, that you intend to leave.
- Follow up with a letter of resignation to your boss.
- Copy the personnel department on your resignation letter.
- Honour the agreed notice period and other contractual obligations.
- Thank your employer for the opportunity they provided you with.
- Avoid burning your bridges.
- Do not make negative comments about the company, your boss or other employees.
- Avoid making any comments about how things could be improved in future.
- Keep your cards close to your chest at any exit interview.

If working in the UK, make sure that you are provided with a P45 form to pass on to your new employer. This ensures that you pay the correct initial tax rate when starting your new job.

You may have outstanding holiday entitlement. You can usually opt to take these days off before you leave. Alternatively you may be given the option to accept payment for them on leaving.

The exit interview

Most companies will organise an exit interview when someone gives in their notice. The employee is interviewed by a member of the personnel department. The employee's immediate boss will not be present. The employee will be asked a list of standard questions. His answers will be noted. Exit interviews are designed to determine why candidates leave a particular job. There may be a pattern in employee behaviour indicating a problem in a particular area. The company may wish to take action in order to reduce turnover.

You are under no obligation to your existing employer to tell them why you are leaving, or where you are going. You may feel it is common courtesy to answer all questions truthfully. However it is in your own long term interests to keep your council. You can be sure that any negative comments you make will be related to your boss and senior management. You may be making these comments for genuine reasons. You may want to improve conditions for your successor and other work colleagues. However you have no control over how this information will be relayed to others.

Your boss will simply take the view that you should have made these suggestions earlier. You may well need a reference from this employer in the future. In addition it is not unknown for employees to return to the same employer several years later. Also you need to realise that your existing boss may well have industry contacts with your new boss. If he passes on any derisive comments you have made it will harm your prospects in your new role.

Occasionally if you are moving to a direct competitor your existing employer may fear that you will take information with you that would harm them. They might ask you to leave immediately and pay you your notice period.

The counter offer

You may well receive a counter offer from your existing firm. This is a common strategy. After all, it is much less expensive for them to offer you say 15% more than to go through the process of replacing you. This would involve the costs of reviewing the job, advertising the role, short listing, interviewing, final selection, induction and a period of training. Even after all this time and expense, there is no guarantee that they will get it right.

You need to consider any counter offers carefully. In some cases your existing employer may offer you a promotion in a different role. It may be in your interest to stay. After all, you have already built a reputation with your current employer. Your existing employer may offer easier career progression.

Bear in mind the following issues:

- Consider your original reasons for wanting to leave your current employer. Does the counter offer rectify these problems? If not, it might be better to move on.
- You have betrayed a certain amount of trust by threatening to leave. You may no longer be in the circle of trust.
- Will you have to go through the same hassle to get your next promotion?

Chapter 39. Applicants from different backgrounds

School leavers or people applying for their first job

School leavers applying for their first full time job often find themselves in a dreaded catch 22 situation. They are not able to get a job because they have no real experience. Yet they cannot get the experience because they do not have a job. If you fall into this category you need to highlight any:

- Part-time work experience.
- Work experience placements.
- Voluntary work.
- Awards such as the Duke of Edinburgh award.
- Membership of committees, sports organisations, bands, etc.
- Computer skills.
- Language skills.
- Transferable skills that might be of use to the employer.

Consider voluntary work as the experience will improve your chances of getting full time paid work.

Sell all of your transferable skills. Even basic work that seems unrelated, such as a waiter in a restaurant, might include many desirable skills such as:

- Punctuality and good attendance.
- Experience of working unsociable hours.
- Maintaining a good appearance and a pleasant manner.
- Organising work routines.
- Dealing with pressure at peak times.
- Improvising when things go wrong.
- Working on your own initiative a lot of the time.
- Dealing with money, numerical skills and honesty.
- Dealing politely with members of the public.
- Dealing with customers' problems.

- Tact when dealing with awkward customers.
- Communicating with others.
- Working as a member of a team.

Employers sometimes worry that younger applicants will have the following problems;

- Less skill and experience.
- Less reliable.
- Less commitment to the firm.

In the absence of any substantial work experience, emphasise personal skills and attributes such as:

- Reliability.
- Dedication.
- Willingness to learn new skills.
- Ability to work as a member of a team.
- Flexibility.
- Enthusiasm.
- Motivation.
- Willingness to work hard.
- Punctuality.

These are all desirable competencies required by every employer for any position that they are looking to fill.

Advantages younger applicants have to offer

Younger applicants often find difficulty getting a job. This is particularly true when they are in direct competition with older, more experienced candidates. However younger candidates offer a number of benefits to employers.

Generally speaking, the perception exists that younger applicants:

- Will accept lower wages.
- Have acquired less bad habits.
- Are more willing to learn, and so easier to train.

- Are more adaptable.
- Are more enthusiastic.
- Are more willing to work shifts.
- May contribute new ideas.
- Are computer literate.
- Have less family commitments.
- Are more willing to travel.

Older applicants

If you have been called to interview, your age is unlikely to have a detrimental effect on your chances of success. You are only likely to have a problem if a medical examination reveals a problem with your health.

There are many benefits in employing older applicants. Generally speaking, older applicants are perceived as:

- Being more experienced.
- Being more conscientious.
- Being more reliable and dependable.
- Being more committed.
- Being more stable and settled.
- Possessing proven track records.
- Requiring less training.
- Having developed better judgement.
- Having better attendance records.

Older applicants need to stress these advantages at interview.

Employers sometimes worry that older applicants will have the following problems;

- Ill health.
- Difficulty in acquiring new skills.
- Less likely to settle in the role due to being overqualified.
- Lower productivity rates.
- Lower motivation levels.
- Issues dealing with stress.

- Resistance to change.
- Reluctance in taking orders from younger superiors.
- Inability to interact with younger colleagues.

If you are an older candidate you need to work hard at interview to overcome these common misconceptions. You need to point out that you will be flexible and open to change. Mention any recent training courses and qualifications to show that your skills are not out dated and that you are willing to update skills.

Older applicants need to practise summarising their answers. They must keep answers reasonably short in order to cover the wider breadth of their experience. They also need to focus on their most recent experience. Industry and management practices will have changed over the years. They must avoid their skills being perceived as dated or obsolete.

Make sure you do not give the impression that you know it all and have nothing left to learn. This will reinforce the perception that you are a little overqualified for the role. It is correct to sell your matching skills. However, acknowledge that you will have to adapt these skills to the new environment.

There is a strong possibility that the interviewer will be younger than you are. You will have to persuade him of the benefits of hiring an older employee. You also need to reassure him that you will not have problems taking orders from him.

Most employers take the view that personal characteristics, rather than qualifications or experience, have more influence on a person's ability to succeed in the job. Concentrate on selling these competencies, as younger candidates are often regarded as being more enthusiastic and motivated.

Women applicants

It is illegal to discriminate against women applicants. However UK management is still a male dominated environment. Equal opportunity legislation is gradually leading towards equality of treatment in the work place. However most surveys show that women are still being held back in terms of payment and progression. Men are still paid more than women for performing the same duties. Women applicants need to bear this in mind when negotiating job offers.

Unfortunately, despite legislation, certain managers and interviewers still believe that, generally speaking, women will:

- Leave to start a family.
- Miss a lot of time because of children's health.
- Leave if their husbands find work in another area.
- Lose a lot of time through maternity leave.
- Have problems dealing with male subordinates.
- Will not fit into an existing male team.
- Be reluctant to work unsociable hours or overtime.
- Are too emotional to deal with stressful working conditions.

As a woman applicant you need to be aware of these potential underlying prejudices. You may have to work harder at interview to overcome them.

To combat discrimination on these grounds firms should use an interview panel with both male and female members. They should also regularly review the intake and progression of women applicants and employees, to ensure that their procedures are fair and objective.

If you are trying to balance the needs of a young family and a career you can consider the following options:

- Part time work.
- Job sharing.
- Flexitime.
- Telecommuting.
- Work from home.
- Self-employment.